HOW TO NAVIGATE THE FIVE STEPS OF YOUR SPIRITUAL JOURNEY

TO EMPOWER YOUR SPIRITUAL SELF!

CHERYL MARLENE

SOUL BRIGHT PRESS

How to Navigate the Five Steps of Your Spiritual Journey
To Empower Your Spiritual Self!

Second Edition

Published by
Soul Bright Press

eBook ISBN: 978-0-9825198-5-1

Audio ISBN: 978-1-945868-49-8

Paperback ISBN: 978-0-9825198-6-8

Hardcover ISBN: 978-1-945868-91-7

CONTENTS

AKASHIC RECORD INSIGHTS

Looking to learn more?

AkashicRecordsInsights.com

Where Inquiry Meets Illumination -- Personal Transformation
through the Ancient Wisdom of the Akashic Records

Akashic Records Insights offers an extensive collection of articles,
new practices, workshops, and workbooks:

AkashicRecordInsights.com

AUTHOR'S NOTE

My life has been filled with journey to places real and imagined, close to home and faraway. In high school, on my favorite bedroom poster were the foretelling words, "Life is a journey, not a destination." As I graduated from high school and moved into the world of college and beyond, I held these words in my heart and mind as both guide and reminder.

The early years of my young adulthood were filled with meeting amazing people everywhere I traveled and lived. Then the motion of my journey would come to a close, requiring a good bye to now precious friends. I was always moving on to new situations, new people, new challenges which I learned would inevitably come to a conclusion at some point. Each relationship had its own rhythm and reward. Each situation offered new possibility and new challenge. But each shift left me feeling forever destined to end, to separate, leaving behind connection and support.

As I continued to move on following the call to the next phase of my life, I began to encounter each shift from a new perspective. I began to welcome each newness as the next step in my journey rather than focusing on the heartbreak of destination achieved only for the purpose of saying farewell. I learned to gather these rich experiences and the gifts of presence from each new friend as the treasured gems of my travels and the crucible igniting new learning and understanding.

Instead of traveling from point to point, I learned to see the continuity joining this step with the next. I began to embrace the *process* the journey revealed, learning that destination is but a beacon which initiates the journey's motion toward unseen, and yet unrealized, possibility. I found that when I allowed myself to move beyond what I thought I knew, I opened to a more expanded perspective no longer blocked by pre-conceived notions and expectations. I realized that the journey moved toward me.

Often this was a scary, unnerving process. While I might write with fluidity now, then was a series of steps forward interrupted by many steps backwards and sideways – anywhere I could avoid the reality of my experience and my own responsibility for my misery and pain. Just when I thought I knew the destination my journey took unexpected twists. I learned that you never get **it** – the journey – done.

Somewhere, I learned to breathe. I also learned about the pointless back slap of demanding self-perfection. Instead I learned about allowing joy to flow unhindered in my deepest being – after, of course, learning that my deepest being existed!

Some of these steps I remember with intense clarity, while others have melted into the flow of my life. I am struck now both by the rightness of each step and the chaos that the journey emerged from and was supported by. What often began as contradiction and obstacle revealed instead synchronicity and a new perspective. I learned to find support in the unexpected and let go of what no longer served me – even if it was releasing the earth-shaking, mind-blowing truth of yesterday.

I know now that I shifted much over the years and certainly now feel more peaceful than at other times of my life. I don't spend a lot of time measuring the distance or the depth of my journey because I try as much as I can to let go of perfection-centered self-judgment. Now I realize that the important part of my journey is what is here in this moment, no matter how I arrived or where I am headed.

Along the way I have embraced the Akashic Records as a source of knowing, healing, and spiritual practice. Through personal experience and a patience learned along the way, I have followed a path I never, ever suspected in high school or college. Though, as I look at my experience over the last thirty years, I see me walking on familiar paths of innovation, research, and sharing with the Akashic Records, much like I did before in other points of my life. As journey, I claim the Akashic Records as guide, support, and fellow traveler.

Interestingly, the Akashic Records is not the only language I speak. The broad reaches of the Akashic Records provide a core which readily translates into many paths, providing access to deep personal and spiritual understanding. The Akashic Records do not require a particular type of belief but rather provide support in whatever spiritual path you pursue. This has allowed me to journey many places within my spiritual searching, connecting with a wide variety of people, processes, and approaches. Rather than limit, the Akashic Records assists me to translate across the breadth and depth of the world in which we live.

In the initial stages of reading and reflection on your spiritual journey, you may experience big, sweeping, powerful energetic shifts of awareness and understanding. Though these motions may also emerge as tiny, nuanced shifts easy to overlook and underestimate. On the spiritual journey, there is room and need for both broad shift and nuanced motion. Major epiphanies can galvanize minds and launch hearts in new directions. Where the seemingly small or minor "epiphanette" can be wrongfully dismissed as insufficient and unworthy. Both have a place, and both help assist in awareness of being stuck and in need of shift, release, and new perspective. Allow. Give attention. Reflect. Let yesterday's truth melt away, leaving room for new vision and deeper understanding today.

Through my experiences I have learned my life's journey is many journeys held within the one journey. Each journey has its own intention, its own rhythm, and some journeys overlap or occur simultaneously. Within each journey there are five discernible steps. Each step has its own primary spiritual concept as well as its own benefits and challenges.

My life as the one journey leads me along many paths. The many paths help me see me and help me learn more about my source: my beginning and my continuing, where I came from and where I go, who I am and who I can become. My journey is many paths along the one mountain of being, here and now.

The mountain is not the destination. The mountain is both origin and creation, both a remembering and a returning. The mountain rises from the infinite and eternal nature of All That Is as the foundation of my path and the foundation of your path and your journey. We all travel many paths along this our common source, seeking understanding, a view of the peak, and the loving attention of shared moments.

Many paths, one mountain, my journey. Many paths, one mountain, your journey. Together, let us begin.

In Joy!

Cheryl Marlene

P. S. This book contains thirty-eight lessons about the five steps of the spiritual journey. Each lesson concludes with a set of questions and an affirmation. The questions may be asked to power personal reflection or may be asked within your Akashic Records. To learn to work with the Akashic Records, check out my signature ***Akashic Records Masterclass***. Because the affirmation energetically claims the essence of the lesson, check out my book ***How Can Affirmations Change Your Life?*** to learn how to incorporate affirmations into daily spiritual practice.

INTRODUCTION

The physical world is the world you can touch, feel, manipulate, and hold. The physical world is thought of as being definable, even controllable because the physical is what is known.

In contrast, the realm of the spiritual cannot be clasped in the hand or logically defined. Beyond control and often beyond your grasp, the spiritual concerns itself with the unknown and the unknowable. The spiritual struggles with that which defies measurement and clear definition – the eternal transcendence, divine motion, God, the sacred, divine source, or All That Is. In the exploration of the spiritual journey, the spiritual is the mystery.

In the journey to understand self beyond physical existence, you begin a search of the spiritual. The path of the spiritual journey leads into the mystery. Little by little examination of the unknown becomes a willing path you choose. In the process, understanding is sought by experiencing self beyond the boundaries of the physical world. This is a journey which endeavors to make sense of the spiritual and the physical together. You seek integration and balance between the demand to know with a willingness to open to the possible chaos of the unknown.

Sometimes this motion toward the spiritual is powered by the lack of satisfactory answers. Sometimes the motivation is a flee from pain and the hope for relief. The mystery without beckons, answered by the mystery felt within. Stumbling in the dark toward the light switch, you find instead a match and a candle to illuminate your path.

Whatever brings you, the spiritual journey is a process, a quest to become more aware of and to expand personal understanding of both spiritual and physical natures. There is struggle with whatever leads to the first step. Initially the challenge is to figure out how to maintain the physical human body as you explore divine nature at the same time.

However, in a more compelling way, your journey must also become a willingness to put the learning and answers to your questions into action, helping you claim your highest expression within the truth and balance of All That Is. The spiritual journey is both thought and action, heart and mind, and always an effort to understand challenges and embrace the best you can be and become. Much more about experience and commitment than goal or purpose, the spiritual journey gathers all spiritual and physical, all experience, belief, and story. Spiritual journey becomes life lived to its fullest. Along the path you learn that there is no difference between life and spiritual journey for they are one and the same. With each step on the path, you claim your journey and live life, knowing that in each moment you embrace process as a way to make sense of experience. Embracing life as spiritual journey is a process which supports each moment of life, encompassing all of life's moments.

Energetic Motion of Your Journey

Often the spiritual journey emerges as awareness expands beyond body and mind. Feeling the deep urgings of heart, the potent call of spirit arises. No longer satisfied with life lived entirely focused on physical experience, personal point of view magnifies, expanding focus, embracing new shifts and new opportunities within life.

Like all energy, inner awareness experiences the ebb and flow of the universe. Sometimes there is clarity, sometimes confusion. Responding to the beacon of inner knowing, you find new awareness and ecstatic revelation, only to experience once again the confusing challenges of daily life. You *deal* with your *issues* only to find that they appear again and again in different situations and in different disguises. Can you ever get **it** done?

In this context, **it** is the search for balance within and without, a balanced integration between physical experience and spiritual experience. This search for relief from the pain of clouded awareness is the spiritual journey, following the layers of soul within the physical form as body, mind, and heart.

Across the entire experience of spiritual and physical, energetically you are everything needed to be engaged with the journey. Over time, The experience of the journey helps release self-judgment and supports choice. Just as the spiritual is not better than the physical, heart is not inherently better than mind, soul within does not trump all. Along the journey, learn to draw upon the best of self, integrating all of who you are with all you can become.

The Five Steps of the Spiritual Journey

To understand the rhythm and cycles of the journey, the five steps of the spiritual journey are a practical approach to the ebb and flow of the journey and of life. These five steps repeat over and over again in each moment, in each day, within all the problems, challenges, and opportunities of life. Layered into life, you may be in the first step on one issue, and the second step on another, and the last step on yet another. Learning repeats itself at progressively deeper levels of energetic dimension. Life's challenges come not to torment with their constant return but because they are the source of your greatest learning and the unfolding of your spiritual potential.

Each step of the journey offers different possibilities for understanding and affects physical being in different ways. Each step holds its own benefits and erects its own obstacles and holdbacks. But all five steps respond through awareness of divine connection and to the energetic motion across the entirety of being. Briefly described here and to be discussed in detail throughout this book, these are the five steps of spiritual journey:

Step One: The Call

Step Two: Preparation

Step Three: Initiation

Step Four: Transformation

Step Five: Integration

What's Your Spiritual Journey About?

To truly understand the spiritual journey and its dynamics in life, first understand what constitutes the ultimate goal. Many think the goal is to get beyond physical existence. Enlightenment, nirvana, and paradise are often all pictured to occur in the pure energy of an angelic, heavenly realm, free of trouble, and most importantly, free of physical form.

Instead, the point of the journey is to learn how to hold physical existence, here, now, while fully aware of and able to utilize and integrate full spiritual energy and understanding. Not only are we spiritual beings having a physical existence, the motion of life is towards full conscious integration of complete being, physical and spiritual, here and now. This integration enables conscious access to the continuum of divine knowing of All That Is as the physical-spiritual beings we are.

Within this integrated perspective, life as spiritual journey is not about getting anywhere. The entire focus or objective is rather arriving at an understanding of truth, here and now in this moment. Getting to truth comes through a process of claiming trust. Trust is the feeling of congruency which happens throughout heart and spirit in recognition of the balance which exists naturally between body and soul within All That Is. Within the spiritual journey, truth is always about balance. Truth comes from recognizing that balance exists and can be felt across body, mind, heart, and soul. On the spiritual journey, reach truth by learning to recognize its flow within your energetic flow. With truth as focus, the spiritual journey then finds direction from intention. An interactive process, journey brings truth and intention. Then truth and intention bring you to your journey.

Your Point of View

Imagine sitting on a train winding its way through the countryside. Through the windows on one side is the view of a beautiful mountain range with snow-capped peaks, alpine lakes, and beckoning forests of towering pine trees. While on the other side stretches the beginning of high plain covered with wildflower and native grass. Each window on the train gives a unique view of the scene beyond, though neither window is better than another. Each window is a perspective, an opportunity to take in a unique view. As the train follows its journey, the view from the window shifts, merging this view with the next.

On the spiritual journey, your point of view uniquely frames understanding and experience of life. Like the lens of a camera, your point of view holds the focus for the spiritual journey. Point of view affects awareness just as the windows on the train frame focus. The direction and the dimensions of focus is your point of view. The broad focus takes in the sweeping landscape. The narrowed focus takes in the concentrated, specific detail.

Always personal, encompassing experience and story, your point of view focuses and influences expression and engagement with your journey, expanding and retracting within the scope of intention, both consciously and unconsciously. The spiritual journey is an eternal process of merging one point of view with the next point of view. This shift in perspective is a progression in general awareness. However, there may not be conscious awareness of each and every specific step nor the exact direction of each step.

Because point of view affects perceptions, your point of view will both clash with and complement the points of view of others. How the self and the world is perceived can be both interfering and creative as point of view inserts itself both beneficially and detrimentally within the flow of life.

Thankfully point of view is directed by choice. Point of view can be consciously shifted in the direction which best serves the journey. Because the entire journey is filtered through point of view, awareness of your point of view is an essential process of the spiritual journey.

The Spiritual Practice of Reflection

Slipping through life missing clues, opportunities, and shifts is easy. The critical voice inside and the people around may yell at you. Together these voices distract from hearing the clear knowing available both within and without. The practice of reflection helps hear and receive knowing above the din.

Reflection:
Intentional focus on awareness in the moment
to learn from and understand life.

Reflection is an all-encompassing approach to becoming more and more aware of knowing, following its trails, embracing its flows. Reflection also fuels discovery and uncovering, igniting remembrance and your inherent ability to learn and to open. Finally, reflection is a process of learning to focus towards deeper and deeper levels of attention, awareness and observation.

Reflection requests attention to awareness whether its motion is trivial or substantial. Reflection pays attention and observes what is going on within and around. Reflection helps avoid knee-jerk reactions in favor of attentive awareness towards meaning and possibility.

Reflection begins with letting go of the assumption that in all cases and in all experiences of life I KNOW – especially I KNOW which comes from a feeling of knowing all and not needing to ever know more.

Approaching life through reflection, begins by admitting that there is much not known. Reflection instead embraces I LEARN. Reflection stands open to receive new views and understanding, to accept the possibility that new knowing is needed and appreciated.

The most important aspect of reflection is what it is not. Reflection is not judgment, not condemnation, not rejection without consideration. Instead, reflection is observation and learning. Where judgment claims value, or a lack thereof, reflection is more like the observation of the fly on the wall, the third-party observer. Taking a step back to observe: what do you see, what can you learn? If there is an immediate step forward to criticize what is seen, you are missing the opportunity for reflection and expanded knowing.

Reflection as spiritual practice open self to more knowing, expands awareness, and allows reception to all that flows to you, through you, and with you.

Reflection connects expanded awareness to the infinite possibility of All That Is. As awareness expands into the unknown, self is no longer reflexively limited. Through reflection, you step into the center of knowing within the infinite and eternal. Because of the importance to the spiritual journey, each lesson in this book finishes with a set of questions to aid personal reflection. These questions activate learning from awareness and experience within the lesson just completed.

Many Paths

Within the joy and the challenge of the spiritual journey there are many paths. There is no one way, but many paths that circle toward knowing and understanding, toward clarity and balance, toward truth and trust. The spiritual path is a metaphor for the movement of universal energy within each individual. Your path on this journey is about your soul's motion within body, mind, heart, and soul. Your path is also about exploration of your personal point of view: where you look, what you choose, how you determine to create and interpret your story. Your path is the motion observed internally and externally. Your path unfolds from your observation of the who, what, when, where, and how of choice.

The metaphor of *Path* may lead you to believe that your path is contiguous, that this step now will necessarily lead to this result and thus this next step. However, what is continuous is your observation and choice, your inscribing of story for yourself. Life is not experienced in neat packages and continuous flows. Often the space between this step and the next will appear quite unconnected, unexpected, and perhaps incomprehensible.

Instead, continuity comes from internal observation and reflection from one step to the next, from one view to another. Your point of view, the stories you tell yourself about who you are, and your opinion about your reactions and choices all come together to influence whether you determine that this lack of seeming disconnection is overwhelming challenge or peaceful, joyous opportunity.

Additionally, no two paths are exactly the same – nor should they be. You may have fellow travelers, but they cannot tell the truth of your path. Only you can come to this understanding for you. You may share experience with fellow travelers. However, your experience of the journey does not give you the ability to determine truth for others. The path may be shared, but each person comes to personal truth on their own. You may travel the same path, but you journey with your truth for and by yourself.

One Mountain

On the spiritual journey, there are many paths. But where do these many paths lead? In essence, the path follows the contours of the mountain set before you. A mountain which can seem literal when life feels like an uphill climb. Yet, in the spiritual sense, this mountain is metaphor for the unknowable, for creative, divine source, for what many will call God. Each step of the spiritual journey leads up a mountain. In the completion of the last step, at the mountain's peak, the next step and the next journey come into view. This next step leads into the valley toward the next mountain, the next challenge, and the next opportunity.

As metaphor, the mountain is the many energetic flows of potential which you create, embrace, and release as you move along the path. This mountain is both a representation of the entirety of All That Is and the many points of view from which the mountain can be seen, understood, and experienced. Let's look at these different views.

Unity (The ONE): First is the awareness of the entirety of the mountain. In this view, the wholeness of the mountain represents the presence of all spiritual and all physical within the unified connection of All That Is. Unity is the one, the origin, the mother, and the point of eternal return.

Duality (The Two): Looking at the mountain from a different perspective, see the connection of the two. Here this duality is called

Potential and Form. Potential is the possibility of form and form is the realized intention of potential. Duality may also be identified as black and white, yin and yang, prana and akasha, light and dark. Additionally, duality is considered as subjective and objective, or as I and not I.

Trinity (The Three): The view of the three takes in the integration and interaction of heart, mind, and body. Other spiritual traditions identify the tripartite manifestation as the trinity, variously named as knower, known, and knowledge; father, son and holy ghost; sattva, rajas, and tamas.

10,000 Things (Manifest Reality): Initially the world is manifested as the 10,000 Things. These 10,000 Things include all that humans create and utilize, including fear and blame, joy and love, both real and imagined. Before starting the spiritual journey, 10,000 Things were mistaken for the entire world, that nothing existed beyond. Through exploration, deeper understanding emerges. Now the mountain offers deeper dimensions of perception no longer limited by the distractive gems of the 10,000 Things.

The Anchors of Your View:

Awareness of the mountain and the many paths is influenced by the anchors of your view: experiences, stories, and choices. Acting both independently and interactively, these anchors may enhance balance and understanding as well as block view.

Experiences: Held within the soul energy dynamics of All That Is, experience is all the internal and external interactions within life in this physical existence. Experience includes all feeling, thought, and sensation, encompassing the entirety of physical and spiritual existence. Experience is unlimited, existing within the infinite and eternal flow of All That Is.

Stories: Stories are the narration to self about experience and choice. Stories attempt to define sense of self, giving birth to habit and belief. Stories can be mistaken as personal essence. However, each story is created to serve a purpose. Therefore, each story may be released when it no longer serves the deepest essence and expression of being.

Choices: Finally, based on experience and story, choice is how you decide to live. In any moment choice is always available, though the choices available are not always what is expected.

Taken all together, experience, story, and choice define personal point of view. The path, the journey, and the perception of your mountain is all determined by your point of view. Seeing beyond the 10,000 Things to the possibilities of trinity, duality and unity are all governed by choice, story, and experience within current awareness and understanding.

In each moment of life, choice, experience and story frame your path and how it ascends and descends the mountain of your journey. Each makes their own way.

Many paths, one mountain: your experience, your story, your choice.

Introduction: Summary

Before you is your journey. Finding your personal path is both challenge and opportunity. Discovering the nature of the mountain is both exhilarating and demanding, peaceful and tense. How you look at the world influences your journey, guides your path, and illuminates your mountain. Body and soul, heart and mind come together to provide support, intention, and understanding to help with this moment and choices of the next step. Though you travel your own path, you are not alone. Spirit as divine motion provides guidepost and connection with fellow travelers and the world. The five steps of the journey help illuminate your journey. Like all things in life, the point is this: Begin. Take the first step. Your life is in your experience. Many paths, one mountain: Your journey is begun!

In this moment, turn attention to heart's depth, and ask self or the Akashic Records:

1. What is the truth in this moment of my journey in this life?
2. What blocks me from seeing the truth of my journey?
3. What gifts come to me from my soul?
4. How does my body help me understand my truth?
5. What is my truth today?

As the journey continues, I affirm:

I am ready to begin.

I am ready to learn.

STEP ONE: THE CALL

HEARING DIVINE MOTION WITHIN

As the journey begins,

Turn attention to your heart.

Listen to the stillness for the Call.

Through heart, soul as divine messenger calls.

1

THE CALL

Took me a while to recognize my journey's Call. I've learned that my call has a familiar feeling which resonates within. Whether I am reading a book or hiking or talking with friends, that place within me sings. The song can be subtle or feel like a loud, clanging gong. Over time I've gotten a bit faster at recognizing the song. I've also gotten better at letting go of the immediate need to know exactly what the Call is about. Now I can hang in the dark allowing the energy of the Call to arise and reveal itself. Challenging to learn, yet patience with myself truly helps.

All journey begins with the first step. The Call.

Softly like a whisper in the wind or suddenly with a force like a sledgehammer to the heart, there is a a nudge or a signal:

Stop and listen.
Notice!
Something worth attention awaits.

This is the beginning of the journey: The Call.

Maybe there is a call to read a book, attend a lecture, or participate in a workshop. Exactly why is not easily understood. Only that something is noticed, is an opening or a receiving. Consciously or unconsciously, this is the reception of the Call, the divine movement of spirit within.

———————

In this moment, turn attention to heart's depth and ask self or ask within the Akashic Records:

1. How may I open my heart to the motion of my journey?
2. How can I learn to hear the Call of my path?

———————

As the journey continues, I affirm:

I trust myself to hear spirit within.

———————

2

OUTSIDE-IN VERSUS INSIDE-OUT

I *remember the day I got inside-out. I was re-reading a portion of Joseph Campbell's book* **The Power of Myth** *and contemplating the idea* Follow Your Bliss. *I was thinking where is my bliss? Inside. Inside me. My bliss is that experience of joy and resonance inside me. My bliss isn't "out there." My bliss is an inside job that I do for me. So simple really when you finally get that it's not about looking outside. Instead the director of my life I find exclusively inside. Any outside source which I find supportive does so because it resonates with me and my inside awareness of my bliss, my happiness, my truth. Blew me away and was the foundation of redefining and living my life.*

As the journey begins, take a moment and look for the focus of your inner personal experience. Is your awareness outside-in or inside-out?

Reacting to what lies outside of self, including parents, family, friends, and society, is a typical way to live life. Learning to define life by what they say is also not unusual. The habit is to orient self to pleasing them. Their beliefs and their motivations become personal. The internal stories of self are based on what they say and explain. Personal experience is interpreted through them and their stories. *I* becomes confused with *us*. *I* exists only through *them* and their illumination. This experience pushes for a look outside self for answers, fulfillment, and validation. In the process, responsibility for life is willingly surrendered to the conditions and people outside of you. You are living outside-in.

Then something happens. Despite their best efforts to maintain control, the joy of self emerges with self, the promise of *Me*, the truth of a deepening sense of *I*. Positive experiences of looking first to self opens a new door. However, the opening is not always positive. Sometimes the sense of *I* deepens in response to disappointment, frustration, anger, and pain, particularly when the answers from the outside do not resolve the inner pain. Nevertheless whether from positive or negative experience, the result may be the feeling of separation from or disorientation with *them*. Their values fall short and no longer serve. There is only one place to turn: to self and self's inner awareness.

To seek understanding within mind and heart, begin a personal search to find meaning apart from *them*. In this shift, personal point of view shifts from outside-in to inside-out. The process of looking first within self begins. This inner awareness begins to find clarity and understanding about the full range of life. Choice begins within, guided by personal awareness and learning.

Without conscious realization this turn inward creates an opening within the heart for spirit to make itself known. With a tug on awareness, or a heart nudge, *the Call* makes itself known in the heart's opening. The inner search for *I* and for *me*, creates the energy within to manifest motion for the spiritual journey and encouragement to take the first step. Life has shifted from living outside-in to living inside-out. Let go of an outward focus. Instead a look within heart and mind seeks answers and fulfillment. Hold you responsible for you. With the inside-out approach, self-responsibility blossoms.

In this moment, turn attention to heart's depth, and ask self or the Akashic Records:

1. How do I look outside for validation?
2. How has the outside disappointed me?
3. How does living inside-out feel like home for my body, mind, heart, and soul?
4. What is my bliss?

As the journey continues, I affirm:

I am responsible for me.

3

BEGINNER'S MIND

I'm a perfectionist who has learned to temper the unhealthy bits. Every time I open my Akashic Records, I remind myself that I am a beginner looking to learn. I don't have to show up perfectly either because of what I do or what I learn. This moment doesn't demand perfection. This moment, and all moments, asks for me just as I am willing to make my best effort. I am here now to learn, to laugh, to live – to begin.

Within the experience of this first step, the Call, the journey's invitation is to explore the spiritual concept of beginner's mind and develop within self a foundation for its practice.

A beginner approaches newness without prior experience and, hopefully, without preconceived notions. A beginner is open to receiving whatever is necessary to successfully learn and incorporate the new skill or the new understanding. A beginner comes to learn what has yet to appear within personal knowing. This is the basis for beginner's mind: an openness to learn, stepping past expectation and preconceptions. In beginner's mind, heart and mind are ready to learn.

With a bit of learning or experience, approaching with beginner's mind can be challenging. Previous study and experience can fool the mind into believing what is needed is already known. Yet this world is dynamic, creating a new infinitely and eternally in each moment. There always exists something unknown, something the heart has yet to explore. Yielding tightly held conclusions to the realm of possibility, allows self to open and receive the potential of the unknown. Instead of limiting belief where all is known, begin by saying, "I don't know." Make a commitment to honor beginner's mind by affirming, "I stand open to learn." Step into the flexibility and vulnerability of beginner's mind. Support the opening of heart. Expand space within to receive the Call.

In the initial steps of the spiritual journey admitting *I don't know* is easier. With progress, do not leave beginner's mind behind as no longer necessary. However advanced the path, beginner's mind is always an essential concept to follow and practice. Beginner's mind allows time and space to consider and reflect. Openness to receive and learn creates the space within to hear the Call no matter the length or depth of the journey. Crucial to the journey is the awareness of stepping away from the direction of beginner's mind. For within beginner's mind, the journey will not be controlled by the erroneous assumptions that all that is needed is already known. Approach the journey always with the open heart and mind of the beginner saying:

I stand open and ready to learn.

Know, however, that beginner's mind is not about giving up self or self trust. With beginner's mind learn to be open to new viewpoints to develop trust and maintain a sense of self-responsibility. Beginner's mind does not give over to outside experts or influences, demanding an outside-in approach. Beginner's mind opens to learn, focused on heart and an inside-out process of truth and trust.

Additionally, embracing beginner's mind opens awareness to the inherent wisdom held in the depths of heart and mind, body and soul.

Beginner's mind opens connection to the best of self and to self-trust and self-truth. Beginner's mind counteracts the closed-off-to-self stance of outside-in and reinforces the beauty and truth of inside-out. Paradoxically, outside-in supports the knee-jerk reaction of I KNOW. Beginner's mind steps past this limitation, opening to the unexpected possibilities of I LEARN.

In this moment, turn attention to heart's depth, and ask self or the Akashic Records:

1. How does perfectionism get in the way of my beginner's mind?
2. How can I release thoughts, feelings, or beliefs which no longer serve me?
3. How can I step into beginner's mind in each moment?

As the journey continues, I affirm:

I stand open and ready to learn.

4

THE FLOW OF SPIRIT

I've always liked the metaphor of river to explore the spiritual journey. The water of the river represents the flow of spirit washing away all that's no longer needed. The river expresses the feeling of spirit flow within. The river is me.

Each person is an integration of three universal forces: the spiritual, the physical, and Universal Life Force. These forces join together to create the center of being from which physical existence takes form and flourishes. The intersection of spiritual and physical begins human expression. Universal Life Force, the animating motion of the All That Is, lifts being from the static into the dynamic, from the linear into the infinite and the eternal.

This integrated balance of the three is connection with All That Is and forms the basis for creating the individual. The concept of *center of being* identifies this central connecting point in balance with All That Is. Awareness of All That Is arises through center of being as a divine presence within the energetic flow of All That Is.

Energetically, another term for Universal Life Force is spirit as motion of the divine. Viewed within the perspective of All That Is, spirit is the motion of divine transcendence. At this universal level, spirit identifies a feeling and an awareness of that which is both connected to self and yet extends beyond today's known.

On the other hand, at the level of humanness, spirit is the embodiment of the unknown and the unknowable. Soul is unique facet of All That Is. Rather than distinct forms, spirit and soul, like all energy, flows on a continuum from potential to form to potential.

Center of being and the flow of spirit are both felt through the heart. Focus attention to your heart to become aware of the motion of spirit within. The outside-in focus leads away from heart and being. Look inside to listen to the flow of spirit within, feeling the balance within spirit that always is.

In this moment, turn attention to heart's depth, and ask self or the Akashic Records:

1. Does my energy flow freely within my center of being?
2. How can I be aware of the flow of spirit within?

As the journey continues, I affirm:

I trust myself to find my balance in this moment.

5

YOUR CRITICAL VOICE

*U*nderstanding the mechanics of the spiritual journey has changed my life. One of the most profound shifts was the effort I made to identify and quiet my critical voice. Quite noisy, bossy, and full of complaint, my critical voice made living almost intolerable at times and held me back from participating fully in my life. This voice made me eat to sooth and pushed me to believe that I couldn't tolerate change and improvement. The vile voice showed up at odds moments and wasn't beyond embarrassment and threats. Of all the improvements I have made for myself the effort invested to still this nastiness was the best investment ever. No magical cures, just a diligence in each moment to not listen, not fuel, not repeat. The payoff: Peace. Peace in my mind. Peace in my heart. Peace in my body. And space. Space to hear and embrace my true authentic voice as deepest heart guidance.

The Call, this first step on the spiritual journey, asks for awareness of the motion of spirit within. There are many obstacles to awareness. The most invasive is the critical voice.

Focused by an outside-in approach, mind can be distracted by the critical voice. Delivered through the mind, the critical voice will make every attempt to distract from the clear knowing of the heart. The critical voice as the flow of *them* will try every trigger at its command to exert control over and keep attention directed to the outside.

The critical voice also hopes to distract by convincing ego to dominate and control life by influencing decisions. Defined as an inflexible sense of self, ego doggedly refuses any effort to re-direct the focus of control away from itself. As such the ego has a vested interest in the success of the critical voice. Beginner's mind is an excellent approach for counteracting the ego's inflexibility, allowing new awareness and knowing to approach.

Instilling the belief that self is unworthy is the critical voice's primary weapon. This sense of lack encourages self to believe preparation is not possible. Without preparation, the necessities needed to respond to the Call are not obtainable.

The next objective is to convince self that you are not ready. Even if you are worthy or prepared, you are certainly not ready to step out of your comfort zone. Your critical voice will try to assure you that nothing is ever worth the risk of discomfort, especially a discomfort which may lead to failure and disappointment. You are not ready. You are not worthy. The risk of mistake is too painful to bear.

Joined together, the critical voice and the inflexible ego try to perpetuate the myth of their dominance by maintaining there is no other inner voice for you to rely upon. This is not true. You do have another voice, your heart's authentic voice. This authentic voice emerges from truth, relying on the inherent wisdom of body and soul, heart and mind. This authentic voice emerges from center of being and is moved by connection with spirit. Because this voice cannot be controlled by others or your ego, the critical voice has a vested interest in questioning its existence and defaming its relevance or connection with personal truth. The critical voice must dominate at any cost including the obliteration of authentic voice.

The critical voice is hard to resist. Layer after layer of mistruth and ill-serving judgments hoisted upon essential self make it hard to hear heart or authentic voice. In the first motion towards hearing The Call, to overcome this resistance direct focus towards the motion felt in heart. Sometimes this motion is easy to spot and, at other times, deceptively small and easy to miss. Practice is required to develop the skill to hear the Call, the motion of spirit within heart, and the authentic voice at center of being.

Know that flexibility is the key between critical voice and authentic voice. Critical voice is rigid, demanding, authoritative, resisting new ideas and learning. Authentic voice trusts your learning process and supports an open, receiving attitude to separate the relevant from the dominating, truth from fiction. Authentic voice helps you step beyond the inflexible NO! of ego to trust heart to make appropriate choices in each moment of life.

In this moment, turn attention to heart's depth, and ask self or the Akashic Records:

1. How can I release my critical voice and allow my authentic voice to step forward?
2. What do I receive from my critical voice which is difficult for me to let go?
3. How can I develop trust in my authentic voice?

As the journey continues, I affirm:

I trust my authentic voice to speak my truth.

6

HEARING THE CALL

Because I lived much of my life in struggle with my critical voice, I remember the day I realized it was gone. Literally sitting on a garden bench looking at the spring flowers in bloom, all I heard were the sounds of the garden, the birds chirping, a gentle bee buzz, a light breeze. Nothing else. No lame accusations, no diminishing comments, no snide observations. I sat a few more minutes and heard another flow: the voice of my heart and the Call of my awareness. The internal fight was gone. Replaced by peaceful, deep awareness. In the quiet, an answer stepped forward like a wave to the shore. Ever since I have been able to hear my Call.

To begin to hear spirit within, first consider the concept of *attention*. Attention is consciously giving direction to your awareness. Give attention to heart and center of being to reaffirm the need and the ability to focus inside self, rather than running outside for answers. Instead, approach with beginner's mind, giving attention to your heart. Many spiritual traditions describe this process as releasing ego to clear the mind. Others describe releasing to surrender the ego's control.

To quit the fight or release resistance, find the spot within where you feel you can just BE. Expectation, blame, fear and judgment (EBFJs) may not be gone, but you will find yourself in a place where they no longer push to lead and dominate.

Now you are ready to *observe*, to take active notice.

From this point of attention within heart, note what your active observation brings to you. Within awareness, observe what moves and what does not move. Observe the source of any motion. Observe your thought and feelings. Observe where you feel open and where you feel closed.

Imagine standing on a beach watching the waves roll in. Observation does not change the waves. Instead, observation follows the flow of the tide and the ebbing of the waves, taking note of motion, direction, feeling, and thought. This is observation of the object of your attention.

Observation leads to *awareness* and supports observation within awareness. Awareness is not about action. Awareness provides the opportunity to gather knowing from observation. By focusing on attention and observation first, new awareness has space to approach and make itself known. Taken together, attention, observation, and awareness allows the flow of All That Is to enter and connect with center of being.

Attention is direction or focus. Observation is actively, intentionally viewing the direction of your attention. You see a little boy crying. You notice a man, dressed in a suit, running. These are observations.

Awareness is gathered from your observation. Awareness includes the knowing, the qualities, ideas, thoughts, beliefs, emotions, and more which become conscious through attention and observation. When you see the crying little boy, your awareness cues you that he is distressed, perhaps lost. The running man has his briefcase and is shouting. You are aware that he is frustrated, perhaps angry, and maybe late.

Observation provides the objective characteristics of attention. Awareness is subjective connecting observation with experience both external and internal. Awareness infers and poses possible meaning.

Another way to distinguish observation and awareness follows the flow of attention. Observation is often about the flow from the outside. In contrast, awareness is attention within. Not separate or distinct, observation begins, and awareness continues. Observation opens outward and awareness is directed inward as conscious gathering. Awareness taps into your knowing.

Paradoxically, the motion of spirit is often found within the awareness of stillness of your being. In the still point where your mind's critical voice has lost its power, where your spirit emerges from your unknown into your known, you can hear spirit, you can open to the infinite and eternal potential of All That Is. Ready to learn, your observation helps find the awareness to release whatever stands in the way of receiving spirit's Call and guidance. With this process of attention, observation and awareness, you open to the possibility of the Call, ready to respond from the love of your heart and the balance of your center of being. Most importantly, you are able to receive and respond to the Call from the depths of inner expression rather than from the distance of outside.

In this moment, turn attention to heart's depth, and ask self or the Akashic Records:

1. How can I allow my attention and observation open the door to deeper awareness?
2. How does my critical voice block inner awareness?
3. How does my awareness connect with my Call in this moment?

As the journey continues, I affirm:

My open attention and observation deepen my awareness of my life.

7

THE ATTENTION OF LOVE

L earning that the quietly powerful awareness that love is attention deepened my life in powerfully unexpected ways. For love has many attributes: patience, kindness, not boastful. Yet as attention, Love speaks to awareness of the whole, the ability to take in the entirety. Love as attention is a heart open without limit. To offer love as attention pulls deep within me and asks that I show up fully, completely, beyond my EBFJs, beyond limit, beyond expectation. Love as attention embraces the boundlessness within so that I can see it, attend to it, and then be aware of the same boundlessness within you. In the attention, love connects me with you, with all, and cannot be denied. That's the power of love as attention.

In the moment the individual soul emerges within the collective experience of All That Is, the awareness of All That Is directs full and undivided attention to the highest and deepest expression of the soul's potential. All That Is observes all that the soul can be and become, and sends this attention in a powerful, energetic flow to the soul. Receiving this attentive flow is your first experience of love. From source, love is the attention of All That Is directed towards your highest and deepest expression. In this sense, love holds complete awareness of your potential, of your dynamic being and becoming, joyfully, infinitely and eternally. Love is attention to the highest expression of your energy's motion. Love is the awareness of spirit's motion both within All That Is and within all that is you.

Beginner's mind leads in each moment to awareness of spirit's motion within and thus to your awareness of the universal love embodied within your entire human experience as body, mind, heart, and soul. Stop and allow self to listen inside. This begins the process of hearing the love of spirit within. By listening, you give attention to heart and center. Attention leads to observation and then to awareness. From the still point within emerges spirit's Call. Giving attention and listening in full awareness to your heart and your entire being is your own personal act for love of you. Listening connects to the universal flow of love and connects you through the attentive flow of love to all other beings.

Listening to spirit within also helps to understand that this process of focusing on the inside first is not actually a new process. As you become more adept at giving attention and observing your awareness, you find that you can rise beyond perceived limits and the impulse to forget your deepest self. In lifting self up, you see and feel that the infinite and eternal essence of your soul remembers and is ready to guide you towards receiving and answering the Call. Never too late to begin, the Call awaits your attention, observation, and awareness of love within.

In this moment, turn attention to heart's depth, and ask self or the Akashic Records:

1. How does my critical voice block my awareness of love?
2. What can I shift so that beginner's mind connects with awareness within me?

3. What is love for me?

As the journey continues, I affirm:

Within Love's attention,

I am fully able to be myself.

I am able to release judgment on myself and others.

8

THE DYNAMICS OF THE CALL

S *tatic and dynamic. The difference between flat and multi-dimensional. The difference between once and always. In my earliest explorations within the Akashic Records came lessons on understanding how energy flows. The static view limits perception to the linear and three-dimensional. Whereas, the dynamic view challenges perception to consider how time and space are understood within the infinite and eternal which encompasses and expresses beyond linearity and dimension. A crucial perspective easy to describe, difficult to fully grasp. In my experience, understanding the dynamic view is constantly evolving, revealing more in small steps of awareness. The main point is to challenge my awareness to not be trapped within the static. This allows me to see dimensions to life I didn't see before. Awareness begins to expand and move beyond yesterday's truth. No longer held back by* what, *my life is focused on the* how *in this moment as expressed by the Call. By learning about the dynamic view, I learn more about me and the possibilities of my life.*

Within the Call is the voice of spirit connecting with heart and mind to assist you in walking the path of your soul.

In a static, linear view, a focus on life purpose appears to be about helping you identify, reach, and live your soul's purpose. In this static view, your life is a train chugging from station to station, hoping to gather all the important bits along the way, often without a clear understanding of what the important bits might be. Both frantic and futile, this point of view will constantly challenge your trust in your inherent ability to find your way. Thus, you think to yourself, "If only I knew my soul purpose, then I would be okay. I could trust myself." This static view can replace self- trust with the need for continual search outside.

However, with the ability to move beyond the linearity of the static view, open self to the dynamic understanding of the motion of spirit within this moment of the infinite and eternal flow of All That Is. It's hard to think about the flow of time and space beyond linear time. Thinking of time flowing like a fountain in all directions is a more supportive and productive point of view. With time moving like a fountain, you are at the center as origin with energy flowing in and energy flowing out, in an infinite number of directions, across the eternal experience of All That Is.

From this dynamic point of view, life's point of support is located within the balance and center of body, mind, heart, and soul. Within the dynamic view allow spirit to come forward. In the dynamics of this moment, the question is not, "What is my soul's purpose?" The question is, "What makes sense for all of me in this moment?" Trust self to hear the answer and receive deep understanding about the dynamic intention associated with your truth in this moment. This is not static purpose. Within the dynamic expression this is how your infinite and eternal self expresses truth in this moment. Each moment of truth connects within you with all moments of truth. The dynamic expression of truth propels you through the transcendent nature of All That Is. Truth is the expression of spirit calling to you in this moment.

There is much that can never be fully known. By connecting with your truth in this moment, connect with the best of who you are and can become, opening self to infinite possibility. In the static focus on purpose, you overlook this dynamic connection of truth.

Very simply, the Call wants to arouse you from a dense fog, clearing the way for you to claim your dynamic soul path here and now.

In each moment of life, you are responding to the Call. In each moment, you are challenging self to be more than you think you can, allowing an inner unfolding within the infinite and the eternal of your deepest, dynamic becoming. Learning to live inside-out brings deep awareness of where you are now and helps you embrace the truth which enables you to move along your path in trust of your truth.

Listen. The Call as spirit beckons your soul embodied. The Call connects you to deepening channels of understanding. The Call asks that you not limit self to what is known or expected. The Call brings mystery and, beyond resolution, offers exploration and reflection. The Call is the beginning and the end. Joyful in its exuberance, the Call begins your journey, offering soul truth and trust as purpose and goal. The Call is you embracing within yourself the one, the joy of one, and the unity of all within and without. Without the Call there is no journey and no reason for connecting with life itself.

In this moment, turn attention to heart's depth, and ask self or the Akashic Records:

1. What makes sense for all of me in this moment?
2. How can I embrace an inside-out approach to life?
3. How can I receive the Call in each moment of my life?

As the journey continues, I affirm:

I am ready to answer my Call.

9

SUMMARY
STEP ONE: THE CALL

I f you get nothing else from this first step, get this: Your focus on learning initiates the flow of your journey. No matter your fears, worries, expectations or assumptions, without learning you will freeze, stagnate and miss the Call. No matter how you might lay the responsibility for an inability to learn on other people, on events or on God, the responsibility of your journey is yours and only yours. The biggest holdback is your focus on the entire journey and not feeling confident that you can complete the entirety now. However, many steps comprise the journey and most steps will not be seen from the beginning. The end may be in mind as you begin, but the steps will shift and change as the journey proceeds. Let yourself off the hook of self-imposed perfection. Let go of trying to see all. Take a deep breath and ask: In this moment, what is my next step? In this moment, what can I learn?

In this moment, turn attention to heart's depth, and ask self or the Akashic Records:

1. What can I shift in order to expand my ability to learn?
2. Do I believe that I can hear the truth of my heart?
3. Is there anything which needs releasing?
4. Where do I feel The Call?
5. How do I hear the Call?
6. How do I allow the prospects of change hold me back?

As the journey continues, I affirm:

I am ready for the learning of the next step of my journey.

STEP TWO: PREPARATION

MAKING ROOM FOR SPIRIT TO DWELL

The Call emerges from within.

Like all moments of sudden appearance,

Prepare heart by clearing space for the silent sound to expand.

Hold heart open, release clutter, gently attend to spirit's motion within.

10

PREPARATION

I RELEASE WHATEVER NO LONGER
SERVES ME.

This is the step in my journey I am most likely to skip. Too quickly I tell myself I'm prepared. I head out the door and I'm down the block before I realize that I shoulda, coulda made the process easier on myself. Before taking a step I've learned to take a deep breath and simply ask myself, "What do I need on my journey?" Time and again hurry just slows me down. I have to remind myself that each step has its own gift to be revealed when ready. Not about perfection, Cheryl. Preparation is about connection with me now, as I am now. Preparation is the can't-skip part of my journey that I have learned to embrace.

In hearing spirit within the Call, the challenge is to prepare room within for spirit to dwell. In this second step, Preparation, the primary concept to embrace is the power of the present moment and the flow of choice available here and now. This process of preparation is also one of inner cleaning and of inner awareness. Letting go of old stories, limiting beliefs, and all that is not essentially you creates space within for spirit to dwell. Learn to love yourself as you are. Learn to forgive yourself and others. See yourself as ready to receive regardless of your condition. Now recognize spirit within and through this recognition connect to awareness of the universal ebb and flow of All That Is.

In this moment, turn attention to heart's depth, and ask self or the Akashic Records:

What do I release to prepare for my journey?

As the journey continues, I affirm:

I release whatever no longer serves me.

11

PRESENT MOMENT

The simplicity of the present moment is easy to dismiss as a popular cliché. However, through numerous experiences of this powerful awareness my attention to the present moment has become steadfast. Focus on the present moment has led me to shift the experience of my life from one where I am in a constant state of questioning to an experience of peace and trust. The here, now. Simple. Effective. Powerful.

The spiritual practice of present moment brings all attention, observation, and awareness to this moment now. This allows access to the depth of being in balance with center and authentic voice. In this moment, all self is present and available.

When attention is focused on the past, life experience is stuck in blame. Whereas fear and worry can glue attention to an anticipated, but not yet occurred, future. Stuck in either the past or the future, you are absent from the center balance of this moment, here, now.

Present moment exists within awareness and choice. Present moment embraces all of self's being and becoming.

Redirecting attention to this present moment, to here and now, brings awareness to the powerful balance of truth within center. At center, is connection to the flow of spirit both as universal motion of All That Is and as an individual, unique facet of All That Is. Through awareness from your center is connection to essence and potential, to fullness and possibility of each here and now. Center exists within the present moment and within truth.

In this present moment is the most powerful place for self because there is access to the entirety of being, all potential and form, all levels body, mind, heart, and soul. In this present moment, attention brings observation of awareness of all of self, making it much easier to see beyond blocks of limiting stories and beliefs, beyond the limit of expectation, blame, fear, and judgment.

Coming to this present moment to observe and decide allows the exercise of choice within awareness. Coming to the present moment within this awareness allows a clear step from this moment to this next moment fully conscious of the possibility of this present moment.

Here, in this present moment, connection to guidance of inner truth is clearest and strongest. Here, now, the flow of divine within achieves its clearest channel within. Here and now is both physical and spiritual balance. Here, now is the seed of the next moment. Here in this present moment is trust providing support for the next step. Here, now is the powerful unity of this eternal present moment for you, of you, within you.

In this moment, turn attention to heart's depth, and ask self or the Akashic Records:

1. How does the history of my past keep me from the present moment?

2. How does fear of the future keep me from the present moment?
3. How can I embrace the present moment clearly and fully, with grace and ease?

As the journey continues, I affirm:

In this moment, I connect powerfully with the best of me.

12

THE GAP

L earning to find the gap between action and reaction changed my life and opened the door to wrestling control over my life from my critical voice. Doubt, space, the pause between breath in and breath out – whatever term used, the experience is the same. The gap offers opportunity to choose within awareness, to live life from clarity rather than the murkiness of knee-jerk reaction.

In the outside-in view of the world, the flash and glitter of acquiring goods, experience, or status can be mistaken as life's ultimate price. Career, family, and life are organized toward obtaining these dazzling prizes to satisfy inflexible ego, social judgment, and the need for outer validation. In the rat race, the self is pushed to the shallow and the superficial. Successfully grasping this objective, the momentary positive feelings push toward another grab. However, ultimately acquisition doesn't improve feeling about self, satisfy ego, or feel the need for validation. Instead, the outward directed cycle continues by another grab after the ephemeral and what will again yield no meaning in life.

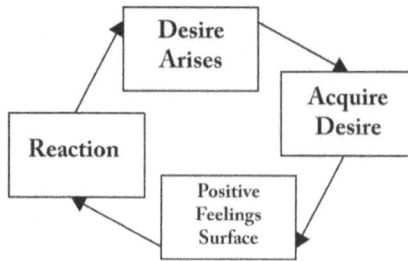

The cycle of desire and acquire pushes towards becoming through a false sense of self identity. A distraction from essential, authentic self.

In this outside-in process, false desire fuels an addictive cycle where motion is driven unconsciously and solely by *reaction* to the attainment of this desire. Disappointment and conflict occur when the desire is not acquired or the expected satisfaction of reaching desire fails to materialize as anticipated. Self is caught in a simple fiction: get *it* to be happy. When the object or the satisfaction with the object fails, reaction fuels the fiction to continue. Response does not question the rat-race cycle following the push to try again to get *it*.

In this frustration of unmet desire, reactions can take several routes. One path justifies the suffering which results from unmet desire. A second path moves to pretend the disappointment did not occur, repressing any feeling, and attempting to gain the desire once more. A third response is self-hatred or hatred towards others. Often denial and hatred go hand in hand as the advance guard attempts to grab the promised satisfaction. Either way, reaction is driven by personal story and belief, by expectation, blame, fear, and judgment. React, then plot new strategy driven by desire and an attachment for rewarding the outside-in point of view.

Driving Force = What

Desire
Arises

Desire
Denied

Reaction
Denial /
Hatred

Feelings
Surface

Unconscious choice based
on Stories and EBFJ

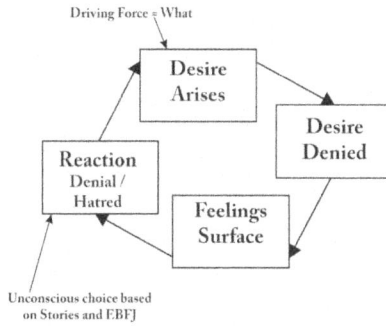

However, in moving toward inside-out process of living, the motivation for action shifts from blinding desire to conscious choice. Shifting attention from blindly reacting to the present moment awareness of center, opens a gap in the cycle between desire and reaction. Focusing attention in this present moment and giving attention to awareness held within heart and mind opens the gap between the surfacing of feelings and possible unconscious reaction. Even the tiniest amount of focused awareness to this moment offers a short pause to consider feelings and whether or not the choice of the next step is conscious or unconscious. The awareness of conscious choice leads to choosing the shape and direction of the path through attentive awareness to heart and mind.

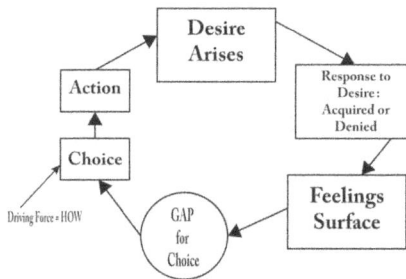

Desire
Arises

Action

Response to
Desire:
Acquired or
Denied

Choice

Feelings
Surface

Driving Force = HOW

GAP
for
Choice

In allowing a gap, habit shifts from the relentlessness of capricious desire toward the possibility, and responsibility, of personal choice. The gap allows action to be based on awareness of feelings and thoughts as well as on the context of the response. Unconscious reaction forestalled becomes conscious action initiated. Attachment to desire begins to lose its hold, turning instead toward the expression of deepest being in this present moment, unique within all experience. Moving from outside-in to inside-out, attention switches from false want to how to live. Life moves from the acquisition of *what* to attention towards the process of *how*.

In this moment, turn attention to heart's depth, and ask self or the Akashic Records:

1. What do I receive from blind reaction in the moment?
2. How can I embrace choice within the present moment?
3. What one thing can I shift so that I can embrace the *how* of my life?

As the journey continues, I affirm:

I allow myself space to move from reaction to conscious choice.

13

STORY, EXPERIENCE, AND CORE ESSENCE

I am not my stories, especially the ones I absorbed as a child unaware that I am the author of my life. Story helps understanding and interprets life events. Not about illuminating all story, rather, I learned that life is a process of releasing what no longer serves and embracing that which supports, in this moment, my deepest being and becoming.

As self-awareness develops so does notice of the internal conversation discussing the nature of self. Preparation as inner cleaning begins by letting go of the limiting stories and beliefs which no longer serve. Observe within self the difference between three aspects of life: experience, the stories self tells about self, and the self's core essence.

Experience includes all internal and external interactions including thought, feeling, and action. Experience is always framed with in a personal point of view. In contrast, story is the explanation of experience. Story builds upon previous story and belief, often elaborated by stories from others. Because story can persist almost indefinitely, story feels refutable and undeniable becoming the illusion of both truth and self-definition.

Stories are created to make sense of experience and of life. Stories interpret experience, develop meaning, and can explain both truth and denial in the moment. Because story can be both positive and negative, the goal is not to rid life of story but to release those which no longer serve or express personal truth in this present moment. Story often holds a static interpretation which may lose its benefit or hide truth. Releasing the static story empowers shift to claim a beneficial perspective of self in this moment of being and becoming.

However, the greatest impact comes in confusing story with core essence. Story can have such a powerful hold that story can be interpreted such that there is no difference between story and self.

Core essence is the deepest expression of soul within physical human form. Felt at center, core essence is eternal, immutable, whole, and clear. Connection to an awareness of core essence can become obscured by the stories created, retained, or accepted in reaction to the experiences of life. As experience creates new stories and new stories prop up new experiences, experience and story drown out the awareness of truth found in the expression of core essence. In the process, self forgets that story and experience are not core essence.

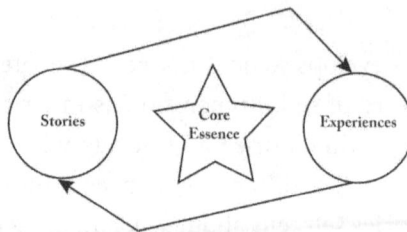

How does this confusion come about? From experience in life, a story is created to explain self, to validate meaning, to temper trauma, or to defend against attack. The story is repeated as truth, forgetting that the story was just an explanation given in the moment. Over time the story is acted upon as truth. More experience leads to more story, all built upon the shaky foundation of stories believed to be unchangeable truth and the expression of deepest being.

However, here's an empowering concept to absorb: story can be changed. Story created in one moment may be released, shifted, and changed in another. Life does not need to be victim to the story of yesterday which no longer serves today. Take a moment to absorb this: story can be changed to empower truth in this moment. Begin by changing the story about your stories:

> *I can now release story which no longer serves me in this present moment.*

Allow the possibility, as well as the responsibility, which comes from releasing limiting story. Feel into center, to your deepest core essence existing within the infinite and eternal flow of All That Is. What serves in this moment may not be what will serve in the next moment. Allow self to move within awareness of this present moment and truth available to you here and now, identifying that which no longer serves, letting go of whatever is not essentially you now.

Life is choice. Choose to release self from a story which obscures core essence. You are neither story nor experience. Instead the truth of self is the essence felt at center. Choice also exists in the explanation of experience which creates story. Story may always be re-examined, released, and reshaped stories so that awareness of true core essence is illuminated.

Story can uplift awareness and understanding of core essence as well as assist understanding of new experience. Thus, life is not about eliminating story. Rather self expansion grows as limiting story is released and replaced by the story of your deepest truth..

In this moment, turn attention to heart's depth, and ask self or the Akashic Records:

1. What stories no longer serve me?

2. How can I see my core essence in the present moment?

As the journey continues, I affirm:

What I tell myself about my experiences supports the best of who I am and can become.

14

CHOICE

F or me, choice is connection to self-directed life. Action, reaction, thought, believe, feeling – all are at choice. My choice. In any moment. Life is choice.

In the journey's preparation, choice is an important component to be aware within the present moment and within the presence of story. Choice, both conscious and unconscious, is the decision to engage with life. Unconscious choice fuels unconscious reaction. Whereas conscious choice fuels self-responsibility. Without conscious choice, life is mindless reaction driven by the cares and concerns existing outside of self. With choice, exploration of the internal and external connections with core essence begins. Through these connections, the movement and support of All That Is can be glimpsed. Truth is found within rather than outside. With conscious choice, living from inner awareness of the essential self becomes more important than blindly following external direction and imposed story.

Within inside-out experience, choice becomes the driving force and shifts personal point of view from *what* to *how*. The focus of *what* is about the attainment of experience and stuff on the outside. Whereas the focus of *how* shifts attention to the process of experience and whether or not choice and action are in alignment with the inner sense of truth, intention, and integrity. The outside-in perspective relieves you of the burden of choice and allows others to make choice for you. However, within the spiritual journey, the challenge is in the acceptance there is naught but self-responsibility. Accept choice first as a necessary burden and, with experience, conscious choice becomes the *how* of life, the way of being.

In this moment, turn attention to heart's depth, and ask self or the Akashic Records:

1. What fears do I have about personal choice?
2. What stories do I have which interfere with choice?

As the journey continues, I affirm:

I am responsible for my choices.

I choose how I live my life.

15

THE OBSTACLES OF PAST AND FUTURE

I grew up with a dinner ritual said just before grace. "The past is accepted. The future is open. Life is here, now." I would mumble along with my family wanting to move through the process to the main event of eating. These days, this ritual has become a powerful mantra and reminds me to pay attention to obstacles to living my life within the present moment – especially blocks from my past and my future which I have created.

The primary obstacle to the present moment is attention diverted to either the past or the future. When experience fails to meet expectations, and attention turns to the past to judge and find fault. In other words, in the sourness of life, past experience ignites blame of self, of others, of events. In blame, attention and awareness are anchored in the past which, however desperately desired, cannot be changed. Stuck in the past, the ability to live within the present moment slips away. Action is limited to reaction and choice is buried by a critical voice dialogue also stuck in the past. When blame becomes so entrenched that present attention fades, life today is rooted in the past. Blame is a bitter weed better left unharvested to wither on the vine. Turning away from blame in denial or deception only creates more resistance to awareness connected to the present moment.

The move away from blame comes in the choice to learn. Blame and the resulting judgment can quickly ignite reaction. However, when blame appears, the opportunity to learn is available by moving from reaction to observation, allowing a gap to appear, allowing opportunity to respond within choice.

Reaction is controlled by the critical voice, the voice that emerges from the powerlessness of the ego. Ego, as an inflexible sense of self, will always urge reliance on outside validation, inciting blind reaction.

Observation as an inside-out experience brings flexibility and possibility. Instead of reacting to create criticism, the gap opens the door to observation by saying, "Hey, what can I learn here?" In observation, the birds-eye view allows sight, feeling, and understanding within the realm of possibility instead of from limitation, doubt, and obstacle. Inner observation balanced with center holds no judgment or criticism. Inner observation integrates the moment of learning with the full force of the soul's highest expression.

For example, when blame controls action, learning comes by following the threads of blame. Bring judgment into the present by saying outloud, "I hold judgment about XYZ." Observe and reflect, examine responsibility by asking these questions:

- What am I getting from holding this blame?
- What does this situation bring to me?
- What am I not seeing that would help me move past this blame?
- What is there for me to learn from this situation?
- Is there anything which needs addressing so I can release this blame?

Insight may explode in one lightning moment or in bits over days or weeks. Let understanding come. Then make a conscious choice to let go of the blame. As always, life is choice.

Paradoxically, releasing blame may catapult awareness not to the present but to the future where fear emerges. Worry and concern question, "What if this happens? What if..., What if...?" Heart racing fear firmly anchors awareness in tomorrow, next week, two months from now – but not in now. Fear and worry divert attention from the powerful truth found in now. Fear is focused on what has not and may not ever arrive. Through choice, acknowledge and move beyond fear to restore awareness to this moment now.

Like blame, relief comes by making fear present. Say out loud, "I feel fear about XYZ." Here that the worry has not happened yet. In this moment, choice and possibility are still available. Now focus is in the moment. See if there is anything to be addressed in this moment about the fear. The question, "Is there anything to do or be right now about this fear?" Take care of anything that can be done now, leaving the rest for the appropriate time. Consciously choose to release fear's hold and move into now.

In this moment, turn attention to heart's depth, and ask self or the Akashic Records:

1. How does blame hold me in the past?
2. How does fear hold me in the future?

As the journey continues, I affirm:

I will not let fear direct my life.

I will not let blame hold me back.

16

FORGIVENESS

Clarity about myself began with forgiveness of myself. Simple to say, challenging to accomplish. The affirmation I suggest at the end of this lesson is what made the shift for me. That and realizing forgiveness and acceptance or not the same. I need not accept to forgive. Instead, forgiveness is simply making the choice to not drag whatever has become the no-longer-needed in my life. I don't need to drag it out or stand as a victim or demand major forms of self prostration. I release. I let go. I forgive myself for forgetting my divinity.

The natural human response to releasing old habits and ill-serving actions is to retroactively penalize self for missteps. Self-judgment can become a revolving, detrimental game. However, the judgment created after release of blame and fear can be more damaging and debilitating than the original "sin." New eyes can see old self with frustration and disgust. Leveling additional blame is the habitual reaction especially in the face of the judgment of shoulda, coulda, woulda.

No longer frozen in either the past or the future, self is now frozen in the never-never land of self-judgment. A judgment which wants to hold self responsible for the stupidity of being less than what is now expected of self. This is a harsh place, a place where motion is difficult. Yet, release is needed and can be embraced through forgiveness as a release of judgment and a perception which no longer serves.

Forgiveness is a conscious inner process of release. Anger, resentment, or disappointment is released so as to not fester within. Within the spiritual journey, the first focus of forgiveness is towards self. Holding onto detrimental emotion and ambivalent feelings especially as a form of punishment is harmful and holds self from the serenity of balance and the release of stress.

As a conduit of personal choice, forgiveness embraces the need for a new vision and understanding of self without judgment. Forgiveness allows motion forward, allows a new sense of balance and wholeness to emerge. Forgiveness allows release from the view of the past and provides a step into a new view available within the present moment.

Forgiveness becomes possible when realizing that the inflexibility of self-judgment is not truthful. Forgiveness as a release of judgment allows the rigidity to fall away, allowing self to stand aware of new possibility, understanding, and direction. Forgiveness lets go of the frozen stance of self-judgment allowing motion forward. To begin a path of self-forgiveness, ask these questions:

- Is now the time to seek (or extend) forgiveness on this issue?
- What needs receiving or acknowledging to initiate this motion of forgiveness?
- How can I see myself in new light? If others are involved, how can I see them in a new light?
- How can I release self-judgment and step into new understanding?

- What is my next step within responsibility, compassion, and love for self and for others?

Forgiveness has its own timing and cannot be pushed. The possibility for forgiveness may appear *before* the time for forgiveness is truthful. However, energetically speaking, release happens only when the potential of judgment has taken the full form of its intention. Allow the flow to bring the gifts and then forgiveness can be a full release of judgment. Forgiveness begins not with a giving but a receiving. Forgiveness receives first and then finishes in providing release. Receive, then forgive.

In this moment, turn attention to heart's depth, and ask self or the Akashic Records:

1. How do I freeze within the self-judgment of prior error?
2. What supports release of self-judgment?
3. What supports the receipt of forgiveness?

As the journey continues, I affirm:

I forgive myself for forgetting that I am divine.

17

THE DYNAMICS OF PREPARATION

W*hen I skip preparing myself, I realize I am being driven by a rush to ignore and deny. I am pushing myself beyond the truth of the moment either because I am afraid or because I feel unsafe.*

Instead when I take a breath, slow to a stop, I give myself a chance to see why I am in a hurry and unwilling to prepare. I learn, I receive, I prepare. Now I am ready for the next step and that will be a much richer experience because of my willingness to have a look-see and prepare.

Remember, please, preparation is not about getting to perfect. Preparation is taking time to be aware of self and to receive and respond within and from the full, wonderful balance of self.

Spiritual practice has the underlying intention of integrating heart and mind within the flow of body and soul. This process of integration creates room within to look at life from a dynamic point of view. Space within self opens for the motion of All That Is to enter and find room. Opening inner space will feel vulnerable. Yet keeping inner space off limits to divine motion creates stagnant pools of fear, worry, and blame.

The spiritual journey carries intention to open room and allow motion. Connecting within opens heart and mind to see whatever impedes full integration. Opening space within embraces full support for the journey and allows opportunity to follow truth as preparation continues.

Preparation is not a one-time effort but a continuous perspective of how to live life. Preparation helps clear clutter and dust from the soul's altar. Preparation supports connection with whatever in this moment allows spirit to enter and dwell. Preparation helps focus, to feel the strength and assurance of connection. Preparation allows the motion of the Call to enter and make itself known. Like getting ready for an invited guest, preparation creates the welcome and ensures the space.

Grant self the support needed to prepare. Without room for spirit to dwell, life is hindered by the shadows and misperceptions of the mind. With spirit inward dwelling, there is room to connect to the soul's dance and welcome the motion of spirit as guide, partner, and divine support. Make room for spirit to dwell and establish connection with soul's deepest, dynamic understanding. Embrace the process of preparation to find alignment and guidance with soul's truth.

In this moment, turn attention to heart's depth, and ask self or the Akashic Records:

1. How do I define preparation for myself?
2. How may preparation assist me in alignment with my soul's truth?

As the journey continues, I affirm:

As I prepare for my journey, I align with my soul's truth.

18

SUMMARY

STEP TWO: PREPARATION

C hoice in this moment is where journey begins here, now. The journey is greatly blocked when choice is neglected because of the unexpected or the unwanted. Claiming choice provides the opportunity to soften the unforgiving stance toward the harsh perception of an error-ridden self. Forgiveness allows reception of all self moving forward fully intact. Mistakes will happen, disappointment will occur. Trying to avoid either at the cost of awareness shortchanges and cripples motion forward. The act of preparation supports choice in this moment, to opening perception to receive and to release. Preparation on the journey opens self to allow spirit to dwell within. Ready for the next step, here, now, in this present moment.

In this moment, turn attention to heart's depth, and ask self or the Akashic Records:

1. What blame do I hold which keeps my attention stuck in the past?

2. What do I get from keeping my attention in the past?
3. How can I release and bring my attention to this moment?
4. What am I afraid of which freezes me in the future?
5. How do I clutter my life?
6. What can I release which no longer serves me?

———

As the journey continues, I affirm:

I am ready for the next step of my journey.

———

STEP THREE: INITIATION

RECEIVING DIVINE GIFTS

On the journey, allow heart the opportunity to dance with the
unknown.

In moments of spontaneity, spirit delivers the unexpected.

Ready to receive,

Gifts come in many packages, most beyond capacity to imagine.

Come these gifts anyway, marching straight for your heart.

19

INITIATION

I n this third step of initiation, move intentionally within the truth of heart to receive the blessings and bounty available by answering the precious invitation of The Call. Standing ready to continue the journey, you willingly open and receive everything necessary: new knowledge, new skill, new practice, new point of view, new way of being. Not that the entirety of the call to journey will be understood, but through truth, faith, and intention, initiation brings attention to what will be needed to complete the journey.

On a spiritual level, initiation appears as the energetic motion of potential begins to pinpoint the clear intention needed to take form within the nudge of the Call. When the Call first makes itself known, intention may remain unfocused or unclear because the Call is more about feeling that something needs attending to than clearly defining an objective or an outcome. The Call brings opportunity to approach in the learning stance of the beginner. In preparation the steps necessary to respond are taken, engaging choice and trust within this present moment.

In initiation, clarity begins to emerge. Within the transition into this third step, intention begins to make itself known. The process of initiation facilitates movement towards greater clarity and self-awareness.

In this moment, turn attention to heart's depth, and ask self or the Akashic Records:

1. Am I prepared to receive a new point of view about my life?
2. How can I trust myself in clarifying intention?

As the journey continues, I affirm:

Intention moves towards me quickly and easily.

20

THE POWER OF INTENTION

I had always thought intention was something so important and valuable that you had to be incredibly careful in the creation of your life's intention. When I could freely understand that intention opens the door to the unknown, I was able to let go of the worry to get intention or perfect. Intention is not about perfection. Intention helps begin and guide the journey, shifting as the experience of life opens new possibilities which come from the unknown – or at least unknown before the journey began. Life isn't one or two carefully crafted statements of intent. Instead intention comes from truth in the moment as assistance to step into the unknown of the next moment.

Intention is the primary spiritual concept of initiation.

From an energetic point of view, intention is always present within any flow of energy. Energy flows from potential to form as the creative impulse of the universe, the movement of the divine, both transcendent and manifest. Within each flow of energy, intention provides the direction to potential, a narrowing of focus which allows potential to become form.

Setting intention is conscious engagement in the creative energy flow of the universe. Without intention life is a ship lost in stormy seas. Intention helps navigate the path and follows the sense of inner truth to find the next step. Intention as a statement of purpose or desire brings direction to conscious awareness. Whether desire is getting to an appointment on time, changing careers, or raising a child, intention focuses attention, observation, and awareness. Through intention, the desired direction is stated to self, to others, and to the infinite and eternal flow of All That Is.

Intention is also the gateway to the mystery, to the unknown. When considering the unknown, or stepping beyond the known to face what is not known, heart and mind open to the mystery of the universe, to the divine unknowable. Allowing this glimpse opens the way to learn, to expand, to enter the soul dance of light and sound within All That Is. Looking for clarity by allowing the gifts of the unknown to move forward into awareness creates a path to expand beyond the limited circle of what is thought to be known.

Common belief holds that clear intention is required in order to proceed on a spiritual journey. This insistence on absolute certainty is a focus on a static, unmoving target. In contrast, when self receives a glimpse of the mystery, the dynamic view appears, and intention is a refining process towards understanding truth in this moment. Intention shifts, changes, and releases within the motion of life. Moving into clear view of intention in this moment will often initiate shift and integration so that new intention emerges into knowing from the mysterious unknown.

As intention is clarified, the direction of life begins to be revealed. If you were just one bit of potential yearning for form, life would be easy as there would only be one direction, one intention. But instead, you are an integrated spiritual-physical container of infinite flows of potential which all arise, following intention, sometimes in harmony, sometimes in discord. As potential within achieves form, more potential emerges. Human beings are never-ending, multiple flows of potential. You are infinite within space and eternal within time, and your journey is the transcendent, joyful desire to participate in the unfolding of the universe, of divine source, of All That Is.

Guided by intention in each moment, you have the opportunity to clarify and claim intention as guide for your journey. From the unlimited bounty, the intention that is right for this moment is the intention which feels truthful, which answers truth, which brings a sense of wholeness, peacefully, joyfully. Intention guides within the great evolving mystery of life's journey.

In this moment, turn attention to heart's depth, and ask self or the Akashic Records:

1. What is my intention in this moment?
2. Is my intention of yesterday still my intention of today?
3. How can I find truth within intention?
4. How can I freely step into the unknown?
5. How is my heart connected to my ability to claim clear intention?

As the journey continues, I affirm:

In every moment, I feel my clear intention open within me.

My intention opens my heart and my mind to the mystery.

21

LEARNING TO RECOGNIZE TRUTH

Love and truth are not separate. Rather love and truth are connected experiences of the heart. Alignment, balance, resonance are the inner experiences which reveal both love and truth. To love myself is to also accept my truth. For in self-love, I give full attention to all of me without reservation or judgment. In feeling truth and love, I witnessed the entirety of me, body, mind, heart, and soul without reservation and with deepest reverence.

In the moment when the soul first emerges as an individual facet from All That Is, the soul becomes aware of the existence of All That Is and wants nothing more than to participate in the wondrous dance, the eternal ebb and flow.

In the same moment, All That Is takes in the awareness of the entirety of the soul and the infinite potential of its highest expression and reflects this attention back. In return, the soul feels the resonance of this divine attention and experiences love for the first time.

*Love is divine attention to the resonating expression of
self's infinite and eternal wholeness*

As soul emerges into a physical body, the resonance of love and connection with All That Is is brought forward into human life. Love is a felt sense born within a human body by the soul's dance within. Love activates resonance.

This exchange of divine love is both motivation and intention and forms the foundation of the soul's eternal support.

Love is giving full and unrestricted attention to the possibility of wholeness within self and within others. Love resonates within the body, mind, heart, and soul, activating all levels of self.

As a beginner in this moment, allow the resonance of love to guide your intention to bring form to your deepest expression. Through love feel the attention that All That Is holds for you as the unique facet of divine source that you are.

Feel and understand love through the primary spiritual conduit, the heart. Heart intuitively comprehends love and recognizes love's deep resonance. This ability to feel love's resonance is the basis of recognizing truth.

Truth touches heart, igniting memories of that first moment of loving, divine exchange, allowing self to forever recognize when love appears. The ability to recognize truth emerges from the soul's ability to give and receive love as unrestricted attention to the resonance of wholeness. Where truth abides, so does love. For truth does not exist without love. Love's eternal support is truth. Hand in hand, truth and love are always expressions of deepest essence, providing guidance and direction for life's journey.

Within this step of the spiritual journey, as eternal witness to love, heart is ready to open to truth. Word, song, action, stillness, beauty, frustration, confusion, disappointment – all of life holds seeds of truth from soul waiting to bloom in the loving quiet of body, mind, and heart. The attentive, flexible openness found in beginner's mind allows you to step forward in this moment to receive the gifts the universe provides to help you find understanding, clarity, and promise for the next step.

Releasing limiting stories, a new perspective of personal identity emerges. Questions arise: If I am not my stories or my experiences, then who am I? Where do I go from here?

Answers come by allowing self freedom to explore. As heart resonance, truth steps forward to guide. Intention begins to clarify: What do I want? What is my intention? How do I achieve my intention?

Truth united with intention encourages acceptance of the self-responsibility to access core essence, releasing anything which may block clear understanding and expression. In initiation, begin to choose your path in order to develop the new skills and perspectives which move the journey in a manner aligned with intention and truth. The direction and the intention claimed follow from personal, inner sense of truth. Flowing from the love in your heart, the resonance within all levels reveals truth. Alignment with truth reveals intention.

In this moment, turn attention to heart's depth, and ask self or the Akashic Records:

1. If I am not my stories or my experience, who am I?
2. How can I open to the truth of my heart?
3. What steps help me clarify intention?
4. Am I able to accept the truth in my heart?
5. How can I recognize truth?

As the journey continues, I affirm:

In Love, I am willing to receive the truth of my heart.

22

THE HURDLES OF INITIATION

P *art of the reason I like to skip preparation is that I like learning. Initiation is where I like to wander, luxuriating in the newly found depth. Well, that is, until I am caught up short by the unexpected. Then initiation gets real and I either have to ignore or deny, putting a stop to learning. Eventually the remainder to be learned pulls me past my harsh self-judgment and blind denial. I literally jump over myself, over the hurdles of my own making. Heart open, now my journey can continue. Yay, me!*

In initiation, the focus is on receiving the new knowing which supports understanding of the Call and its emerging intention.

This process of receiving can be quite joyful as the new perspective opens up new vistas and new understandings. However, there are also many challenges which will arise and attempt to halt any efforts. The ugliest is feeling unworthy, feeling incapable to learn or embrace the new perspective. There may also be feelings which cannot be fully processed or understood and thus releasing blocks doesn't feel possible. Overwhelming feelings may drown out other emotion, leaving self feeling empty and pointless. Simply put, you may feel too small for the tasks of the journey.

Amazingly, this is both a common feeling and a helpful feeling. As low self-worth feelings emerge, you are being shown what needs attention, what needs release, what needs love within your body, mind, heart, and soul.

In the initial motions of the journey are the beginnings of learning all that is needed to fully receive the gifts of initiation. However, this is the point of initiation: guidance through the process of learning and opening to receive all that is needed to continue the journey.

Pay attention, therefore, to what brings these feelings of inadequacy. Within these feelings are the seeds of acceptance ready to be planted. Realize the ego would like to avoid this expansion. Know that not moving forward can be its own form of vanity. Instead, look to your heart for guidance and truth. You are worthy of your journey and it is up to you to choose how you will engage—or not.

Paradoxically, sometimes the journey's learning process requires a release or an unlearning of yesterday's truth. This feels disruptive. Not only was that understanding hard won yesterday, often the pressure for release comes before clarity of the new truth. You feel pushed to release but don't yet know or understand the newer truth which is just beginning to emerge.

In learning to receive the new, first release the old because the new and the old cannot be held at the same time. Like someone trying to catch the flutter of papers in the wind, you may feel yourself desperately running here and there, grasping and missing, grasping and missing. Instead of chasing something on the outside, the answer lies with your heart: What is my truth now?

Take care of whatever can be attended to in this moment, trusting self to attend to the rest in the appropriate time. This helps release what does not serve now and creates room for new truth to appear when ready. Let go of the demand to clearly know the new direction before letting go of the old. Offer support first to create space within for the soon-to-come, now emerging truth.

The process of initiation can also tug and push at a sense of self-complacency. Life may feel fine just where you are, feeling no great need to take on new perspectives or push into new territory. This can be particularly true when you still are not certain that the Call is for you. If this is the case, take a moment to look at your life. Examine whether this potential direction is truthful in this moment. Pushing yourself to do something without a clear sense of commitment is not productive.

At the same time, realize that the nudge of the Call may be trying to shake lose a stance which no longer serves. Looking inward for a sense of balance will help you take a hard look at self and whether or not you are stagnant or standing in the inflexibility of harsh self-judgment.

Initiation may also be pushing at your inflexibility—a stance encouraged and protected by ego. Energetically ego is inflexibility, an inability to allow self to grow and expand beyond rigid self-definition. Learning pushes at these hardened boundaries. To control and direct, ego tries to lock down thoughtful response and encourage fearful reaction.

Unworthiness, self-complacency, and inflexibility are all part of the same challenge. Each, in its own way, want to contain and hold you back, while limiting personal growth. However, to take on the new skills of initiation, a receptive perspective is required. In this moment, the journey asks you to absorb all that supports your efforts in this step to truly create a new beginning. The Call continues to move you toward a new view of self and self-expression. And now, in initiation, you are receiving, allowing spirit to bring forward that which responds deeply to the Call.

Whatever form initiation may take, the experience will be both expected and unexpected. New ideas, new skills, new viewpoints, and new knowledge are all possibilities within initiation. Whether initiation is attending a workshop, reading a book, hearing stories of yesterday from a loved one, listening to the bird singing outside your window, or a serious discussion with a friend, your experience will be more than initially imagined. Through the open awareness of beginner's mind, the path presented within initiation will step forward in a completely unanticipated form. Whatever is presented, recognize your path through the resonance of truth. Initiation answers the call of the heart to receive whatever spirit brings forth. Initiation sounds within as loving impulse to be completely open to the flow of being and the motion towards highest expression. Initiation answers the Call because you are prepared and ready to move within the balanced flow of your awareness and openness.

The process of initiation also begins to clear the clutter of the no-longer needed, strengthens the heart's ability to receive, and enables the mind to find comfort and truth through new learning and new awareness. Initiation is a beginning which strengthens the platform of the journey and brings sustenance to move forward. As personal energy level begins to rise, you may feel a positive upliftment into new vistas and new visions. Intention is clarified, bringing a sense of truth to this step and the next. Initiation brings focus and an ability to move in trust, ready to see the journey unfold within all of you and within All That Is.

The last challenge of initiation is this one word: Why? Why am I taking this class or reading this book?

Initiation does not need to answer the question of *why* in order to achieve its intention. Sometimes why is understood, maybe even from the first awareness of the Call. Not knowing why is just as likely while still have clarity that, for whatever reason this path, these steps are the right ones. Or over the course of the journey, the first *why* may fade as a new *why* emerges. Come what may this is life and you cannot imagine holding yourself back. The only choice now is your journey's next step.

In this moment, turn attention to heart's depth, and ask self or the Akashic Records:

1. How can I be open to receiving new knowing as I take on the new skill of initiation?
2. What supports me in releasing yesterday's no longer supportive truth?
3. How can I become more flexible?
4. What is the energy of the unexpected in my life?

As the journey continues, I affirm:

I no longer hold back from the newness of life.

I eagerly receive the gifts of initiation.

23

TRUST

The pain of my early life made it hard for me to trust myself. The stories held about me by others threatened my personal sense of trust. Yet, as a I leaned into me and what I perceived truth to be for myself, I began to see that the pokes at me by others were actually opportunities for me to learn to trust myself. Lemons to lemonade, I learned my ability to trust of myself was intrinsic regardless of what others said. Covered sometimes by life's dirty moments, but there, nonetheless. Trust, in my heart, always.

Within the spiritual journey, the courage to follow truth is found by claiming the support available through trust.

Trust is the willingness to take a step forward not entirely aware of the entirety of truth — even though anxious to do so, even though new clarity has yet to emerge. Trust is a conduit between intention and truth which helps move life in the direction that *feels right* even though you do not completely comprehend why.

This spiritual journey, this ebb and flow of life leads away from the controlling, must-always-know-why orientation of mind to the trusting, inner knowing of heart. Mind can get caught in the web of cause and effect to the extent that nothing in life is completed unless there is absolute certainty about where a particular step or path will lead.

Additional exploration of the spiritual within helps find threads of contact with divine connection and its unfailing, unconditional support. This contact touches and further opens the room in your heart, allowing greater awareness of and access to the divine knowing of the soul. In turn, you become more capable of asking for guidance within, following its gentle nudge, and allowing the joy of the moment to unfold, revealing spirit's gifts and powerful soul guidance.

Trust comes as experience of life supports your inner work. Releasing the pressure of the critical voice, opening heart to the resonance of truth, staying with self-awareness within the present moment – all of your effort builds your ability to trust you. Small steps, one step at a time all lead to trust built consistently over time.

Trust and the guidance of intention are made known in the loving embrace of truth and love. On the spiritual journey, begin to follow this heart path to learn to trust the Call's wisdom even when you cannot explain why.

The form and content of initiation take shape within the experience of recognizing truth and following the directed feeling of intention. Trust and self-acceptance reinforce the trust of truth and intention within the deepest expression of body, mind, heart, and soul. Initiation refines the abilities of attention, awareness, and observation and, together with truth and intention, encourages trust that the next step is taken in alignment with your soul's call.

Again, at its deepest levels, initiation is not so much about **what** you do, but the process, the **how**, to come to understanding truth and intention as experiences of divine love and personal truth.

Initiation is receiving. At deeper levels, the focus of receiving moves away from a focus on the content. Instead, focus moves to the process of receiving. Blocks emerge from an unwillingness to release an idea or belief that once was true but no longer serves. Many spiritual traditions speak of surrender at this juncture. However, the crux of the issue is to challenge self to be open to learn no matter where you are on your path. Whether you surrender or lean into learning, trusting self is the primary focus.

In openness to receiving, initiation guides towards a path of truth and understanding of soul's intention. Be here, now, prepared to receive and release. Trust that you will always have the knowing needed to receive your call. Allow the clarity of intention to guide in finding the next step in this your amazing and joyous life.

Trust develops and emerges from within. Baby step forward, giant step back as you test out your ability to listen and trust the motion of guidance within. In focusing on the *how*, trust has the opportunity to emerge from the depths of who you are and who you are becoming. In turn, this allows your ability to trust to deepen and build over time.

Most importantly, trust supports in bringing self to center where you can hear your authentic voice, touch your core essence, and focus on your heart as a source of trustworthy guidance. Balance always is. Within is an inherent wisdom hidden by the critical voice and ill-serving stories. In receiving the gifts of spirit, you receive you, connected, whole, and full of love for life.

In this moment, turn attention to heart's depth, and ask self or the Akashic Records:

1. How can I open to receive?
2. What is trust for me?
3. How do I open my heart to trust?
4. What blocks my ability to trust?

As the journey continues, I affirm:

I trust myself deeply and fully.

24

THE DYNAMICS OF INITIATION

*I*f there's only one idea to fully understand about your spiritual journey, it is this: you never get the journey done. Why? Because your journey is your life. Each moment of life is journey. Not only a work in progress but also an experience in each moment which animates life beyond into the omnipresent connection with the divinity of all. Each moment is initiation within this omnipresence. Within initiation, the heart hears, the eyes welcome, and the mind connects with the depth of life now and however becoming manifests in the next step of life's journey.

Honor self by honoring your personal process of embracing new truth and understanding.

In each moment of living, open your entire being to embrace new learning.

This newness is crucial to the expansion and growth of your entire being. Without the new perspective of the shifting, ever-changing motion of All That Is, each view of your journey would be the same, time and time again.

The power of your journey emerges not from repetition but with divergence from the expected. Allowing self to be initiated in each moment, allows you to witness the new motion, the new thought, the new feeling, the new sensation. At its core, the spiritual journey is precisely about this process of allowing the previously unknown, but now emerging, to become part of personal knowing.

Stepping into the process of learning allows this expansion within each moment of connection. Initiation receives the gifts of being and becoming openly and expansively. Initiation is reception. Initiation embraces newness as the path from this moment to the next. Initiation receives the promise of the Call's mystery and allows the unfolding to continue.

Within your journey, initiation is both process and point of view, both an allowing of new understanding and an embracing of unknown possibility. Initiation begins to process the Call's journey within the perspective of your soul. You are learning to allow the unknown flow, and to allow new understanding and new joy to emerge for you and within you.

Initiation as both continuation and deeper revelation, supports the journey and holds promise of genuine understanding. Here, in initiation, the depth of process begins to reveal itself and begins to help you move beyond the limits of yesterday's beliefs and yesterday's truths.

Initiation helps plot a new possibility, a new path toward yet unseen vistas. Initiation brings the understanding needed to feel the possibilities of truth and the possibilities of staying true to the entirety of self – heart and mind, body and soul. Initiation prepares the journey and compels both truth and motion. Unstoppable, embrace life as both spiritual practice and spiritual journey to deepen the capacity of your heart and live within the deep meaning of your soul.

In this moment, turn attention to heart's depth, and ask self or the Akashic Records:

1. How does the process of initiation show up in my life?
2. Am I open to learn?
3. How can I open myself to the newness of my spiritual journey?

As the journey continues, I affirm:

I am open to receive all the possibility of my life.

25

SUMMARY
STEP THREE: INITIATION

The promise and the challenge of initiation is receiving. Overly focused on giving or "being in service," this tightly held focus will interrupt the entire process of initiation through either misunderstanding or a complete dismissal of initiation's necessity. For there to be an ebb and flow in life, you need more than ebb, giving. Find a way to allow flow, being open to receiving, then the next step is to feel balance between the two. Without balance, the necessary elements of your journey will be difficult to find. Life will stagnate and motion forward will halt. Receive. Receive the gifts that the universe brings. Receive awareness. Receive trust. Receive truth. Receive self, balance, and love. Receive.

In this moment, turn attention to heart's depth, and ask self or the Akashic Records:

1. How do I feel unworthy?
2. How do I experience Love?
3. How do I hold myself back from Love?

4. What do I get from avoiding Love?
5. When I look in my heart, what do I feel about my ability to trust myself? Trust others?
6. What shifts will best support my ability to receive?
7. How do I get in the way of my receiving?

As the journey continues, I affirm:

I embrace the gifts of initiation with an open heart full of trust and possibility.

STEP FOUR: TRANSFORMATION

LETTING SPIRIT GUIDE

On the wings of silent offering come the possibilities of a million worlds.

Take heart and open.

Within the Call is invitation to fly in tandem with the Divine.

Don't mistake this peak as the final one,

lest you miss the journey all together.

26

TRANSFORMATION

Transformation, I learned early on, is not the be-all-end-all of the spiritual journey. However, transformation is absolutely necessary to get anywhere in life. Can't skip, ignore, deny, or trade away for magic beans, transformation is the gotta-do. Without the previous three steps, transformation is flat and superficial. One step at a time, giving each step equal attention sets the stage for transformation that will knock your socks off with the gentle brush of a butterfly's wings.

Spiritual transformation is often described as the primary goal of spiritual activity. *Change yourself, feel the power of transformation, step into a new you!* Sound familiar? Before you read any further, please stop. Breathe deeply in and out. Let go of everything you think you know about transformation. Bring forward beginner's mind and move into a place where you feel comfortable asking, "Transformation – what's that?" Ready to begin?

As the fourth step in your spiritual journey, Transformation is not the end game. Transformation is not the destination, not the goal, not the conclusion of any spiritual journey. Transformation is not about fixing you. Transformation does not eliminate the problems or disappointments of your life. Transformation does not ensure paradise nor come with a guaranty of any kind.

Instead, Transformation occurs in the moment of releasing limiting stories, judgments, and fears. When you willingly allow self to stand in that vulnerable place of observation of all warts and disfigurements. That place where judgment and blame lose their hold. Where you step right into fear, and set intention by declaring to the universe, "No matter what happens or what is required, I live my truth in this moment!" You move beyond what no longer serves you, releasing the unessential, stepping into learning and opportunity. Not because pain will be relieved. You let go to receive because the pain of feeling self separated from deepest truth has become unbearable.

Transformation begins in the moment of risking all to come face to face with the powerful truth of deepest being. You willingly risk facing the possibility that your stories, judgments, and fears may all be completely true and entirely false. You take this risk for the possibility of a clear vision of core essence. Transformation is the moment of finally arriving at the peak of the journey's mountain and feeling shift within. In this moment, the shift brings a sense of clarity, a feeling of balance and openness, a receiving and a releasing.

Transformation occurs when, all of a sudden, the unknown leaps unexpectedly into your known. It's the Ah-ha! moment of feeling a shift, a letting go, and an embracing. Within this transformational motion there is awareness of cycles shifting, paths opening, knowing unfolding. Within transformation, you feel, "I am the same person never to be the same again. I am a new me."

Paradoxically, in this moment of risk, the fear is not of being a miserable failure. Instead, the worry is that you are powerful – powerful beyond fear, powerful beyond hope and dream. As the Call shifts knowing into an awareness in this moment of the awe-inspiring potential of All That Is, you instantly flash on the wonder of your wholeness, of your balance, peace and joy, in this moment, powerfully here, powerfully now.

Transformation touches your core, vibrates with the powerful essence of being, and embraces the potential of becoming. In risking failure, transformation helps release the fear standing in your way, yielding the clear view of the true depth and power of your being and becoming.

———

In this moment, turn attention to heart's depth, and ask self or the Akashic Records:

1. What preconceptions about transformation does it serve me to release?
2. What limiting stories, judgments, or fears create blocks to the fullness of my life?
3. What is the spiritual perspective of personal power for me?
4. How do I block the best of me from fully accepting the wholeness of my life?
5. At the core essence of me, who am I?

———

As the journey continues, I affirm:

Claiming all of me, I step willingly into the light of my deepest being —
and see myself.

———

27

THE ENERGETICS OF INTEGRITY

I ntegrity surprised me because I used to think of integrity as a single destination. Release and get there, I thought. I am an honest person, of course I am in integrity. But as the arc of the spiritual journey is never done, integrity has many layers to release and to embrace. Integrity then is another gift of awareness of balance and imbalance, of alignment and resistance, of possibilities within push and pull.

In this fourth step of the journey, balance at center is felt as truth and expressed within the spiritual concept of integrity. Energetically, integrity is the awareness in this moment of how the motion of life intersects with intention and action. Thus, integrity yields a sense of balance within all aspects of self. In contrast, being out of integrity is the awkward feeling that something is out of place somewhere in life's experience. Sometimes the exact culprit of imbalance can be identified while at other moments there is a vague feeling that shift is required.

Integrity, often identified as honesty, is also the state of being complete, undivided, whole. Integrity with self allows and encourages a step into the vulnerability, risk, and powerful shift of transformation. From a spiritual energy perspective, integrity is the conscious intent to maintain balance with the experience of center connected always to All That Is. Integrity is the conscious intent to live life in balance with truth at the deepest and highest levels possible.

In day-to-day life, integrity is the commitment to being your word. You do what you say, and you notice when you do not. In integrity, you are present to and attentive to the promises and commitments made to self and others.

Because integrity exists at both the levels of form and potential, holding self back from a full experience of life in order to never break a promise or miss a commitment is limiting self to the mere shadow of integrity. Instead of full commitment to life, this is an illusion of control geared towards an idea of perfect spiritual practice. Living life in predicted perfection, attempting to control events to always be in integrity is an insidious form of denial. Single-minded focus on perfect action is not wholeness and is not of integrity.

The essence of integrity steps forward when deeper understanding brings awareness that full integrity is not simply the perfect completion of each and every commitment. Shift happens. In the motion of life, integrity is the self-responsibility that steps forward when realizing that for whatever reason you are not keeping your word. You move to take care of the consequences. Understand that integrity is the entire flow between the feelings of balance and imbalance within your center and the ebb and flow of All That Is. This provides the perspective that integrity is less about *what* you commit to and more about *how* you engage with your commitments especially when the commitment cannot be kept as originally made.

Remember that the static doingness of mind leads to the belief that perfect action is the goal. Being somehow less than perfect in commitment and action, you may mistakenly believe the myths of your brokenness and your imperfections. In transformation, face to face with the totality, you realize that you come to this Earth in wholeness. You are whole and life is a cycle of contraction and expansion, an observing and a remembering, a being and becoming.

You do not need to fix yourself because you are inherently whole and unbroken. Instead, in the process of living, continually rise to a point of awareness where you see and experience your divine whole, within the entire continuum of being. Claim body, mind, heart, and soul as one integrated, transforming whole.

The human experience in its deepest expression is a transforming integration transcending the separation implied by using the words *spiritual* and *physical*. In transformation, feel your wholeness at one with All That Is. Whether a fleeting glimpse or a life-changing, irresistible shift in conscious perspective, transformation is a receiving that cannot be denied, a receiving which flows with truth, love, and joy.

Additionally, understand the spiritual journey as a spiral dance across the experience of life. Envision your journey as a cycling of steps across the mountains and valleys where your path leads. Each of the five steps of the journey are repeated over and over, bringing new awareness and understanding each time.

Transformation is also an experience which is repeated over and over again in a variety of different ways within a multitude of issues and challenges. Sometimes transformation is a big *whoo-hoo* of joyful realization. Sometimes transformation is subtle, nuance of shift. But in that miniscule shift, is the experience of profound motion. Sometimes, the seemingly insignificant offers the biggest Ah-ha!

Transformation can be quick, blunt, and overwhelming. Transformation can also be gradual, slow, building over time. Sometimes you experience a major shift where one day everything in the world appears black and white, while the next day life shows a million colors. In one swift motion life shifts radically. Prior to transformation there can be powerful feelings of exuberance in the letting go that precedes. There can also be a heart-rending feeling of sadness in finally releasing whatever has been held to so tightly. Contradictory, transformation is both a falling apart and an amazing weaving together of potential and form.

However, transformation does not require radical change in any direction of doingness. Transformation ultimately is a shift in perception and awareness, and in the connection with inner knowing. It's about clarity, about clicking into the channel which eliminates static buzz within awareness.

Frustratingly, it is not possible to predict what will set off the Ah-ha moment. The where, the how, or the when of transformational shift is not predictable. You may be able to feel yourself building toward the moment, but you can't predict when the energetic shift of transformation will happen. Like a surprise gift, the moment of transformation comes when least expected. Integrity brings the wisdom needed to acknowledge the shift when trust engages within body, mind, heart, and soul.

In this moment, turn attention to heart's depth, and ask self or the Akashic Records:

1. What is integrity for me?
2. How am I not honest with myself or others?
3. What steps can I take to bring myself into integrity when I am not at my word?
4. How does perfection cause me pain in my life?
5. How can I feel safe within the unexpected?

As the journey continues, I affirm:

I open my heart to the unexpected.

28

CONSCIOUS INTENTION

For me both the thrill and the burden of embracing my life as spiritual journey came with increased awareness. Expanded consciousness reveals the beauty and wonderful wonder of life. Each moment experienced within all. At the same time, clear vision reveals warts and bruises and all that you feel is lacking in perfection and value for yourself. At first, this consciousness is overwhelming and can be disheartening. How will I ever get it all done? With a few more steps, I realized I don't ever get the journey done. Focus in this moment allows me to be aware of balance and integrity in this moment. With conscious intention, life happens in this moment. Imperfections don't magically resolve but in this moment, I can resolve what needs attention in this moment, consciously and within the deep sense of me as conscious being.

Living consciously is expanded awareness of motion within and around self. Expanded awareness of integrity fuels awareness of intention and how both emerge from inner balance. With deepening awareness of balance comes the ability to observe at deeper levels the motion of inner awareness. A powerful feedback loop energized by the impact of transformation.

The shift of transformation opens new doors, revealing new ways to view and understand both the journey and life. Instead of yielding to reaction and blind response, you begin to bring awareness to intention and to the possible directions of life. Initially, the Call helps find the ability to prepare self and to initialize learning so that you may willingly find balance with self and with All That Is. In the transforming moment, you come to the pinnacle of this awareness and experience truth within.

Conscious intention allows balance and truth to guide choice and action. Conscious intention, fueled by awareness of personal intention and the balance of integrity, embraces the guidance of motion felt within and without. With conscious intention, self is fully present within the shift of transformation in a new direction with new awareness of life's unfolding potential.

Integrity lives within conscious intention to find balance through awareness of truth. Integrity experienced daily is truth consciously lived daily. Integrity as balance is the knowing of truth both as inner peace with self and the joyful awe of glimpsing the infinite and eternal of All That Is. Whole, undivided from being, integrity fuels awareness and ignites the Ah-Ha! moment as a recognition of wholeness and completeness felt as peace, joy and balance.

In this moment, turn attention to heart's depth, and ask self or the Akashic Records:

1. What steps can I take to live life with conscious intention?
2. How am I open to new awareness and understanding?
3. Within, where and how do I feel balance?
4. Am I ready to accept truth?

As the journey continues, I affirm:

I am connected with my awareness of balance and truth in this moment.

29

BREAKDOWN VS. BREAKTHROUGH

I used to have major panic attacks which I have since been able to understand and resolve. However, at first, the resolution didn't help me with the habit of breakdown. Caught in the worry of being less than perfect, as my life shifted, I would have moments of pure panic that my life was permanently falling apart. I lived and breathed breakdown. Until one day, in a "Duh!" moment, I realized I wasn't falling apart. Instead, I was moving through. Deep breath! Follow the motion, I told myself. Like the caterpillar become a butterfly, in this motion is not disruption. Quite the contrary, in this motion I embody transformational focus.

With the approach of transformational shift, the unknown comes closer and closer. Like any challenge along the journey, the critical voice can still be overwhelming. The ego does not like change and is frightened by the unknown. The shift of transformation can feel too bright, too daunting, and the sense of no-turning-back can be overwhelming. Something within may want to turn around, saying, "Hey, I was only kidding. This is too much! Yo! Not what I signed on for!" Returning to the darkness may feel like the best choice. You may even feel tempted to deny the transformational moment because looking the unknown in the face can be difficult. Life feels as if it is breaking apart.

These feelings of breakdown are fueled by feelings of unworthiness and fear. In breakdown, self is distracted by the *what* of life. Focus is frozen on actions, behavior, doingness. Focused on doing allows the mistaken belief that there is nothing unknown in this moment. Doing attempts to banish the unknown. Yet unknowingly, transformation has brought the moment where one form is released while another emerges. Feeling into the unknown of this new form can feel like life is coming apart. Challenge is everywhere. There is struggle trying to keep life together. This is the experience of breakdown: the fear of a completely, irreversibly falling apart of your entire life.

You are right – and wrong. Within transformation, there is no going back, but you are not breaking down. The experience is breakthrough. In the face of the unknown, motion may feel wrong. However, in the perspective of the soon-to-be known, you are moving through into a new way of being, into a new view and new understanding of your entire life.

Not down. Not out. Not away.

Through.

You are moving through what no longer serves into the unfolding, emerging unknown that is your truth, here and now.

Confusing outer world goals as those only worthy of attention and focus will trap self in constant doing. To-do lists and five-year plans are helpful only as long as they do not distract from the larger picture of the truth, intention, and integrity of being. Doing can be part of or even a trigger for an awareness of being. Yet, doing can also become a confusing distraction chosen because you want to stay put and enjoy the comforts of the known rather than the possible breakdown anxiously offered by the unknown.

In contrast, being encompasses all of you, all experience, all feeling, thought and action. Being is the entire spiritual-physical expression of you as a unique facet of All That Is. Doing is only a small part of your entire expression. What you do may in part guide your focus, but *how* you live defines and is defined by intention, guided by and guiding integrity.

Getting to the supposed end of the journey is a focus on *what*. Being present to each and every moment of the journey is the expression of your being, the *how* you choose to live your life. In the *how* of life, consciously receive the gifts of life and, through observation and attention, come to an awareness of intention and deepest knowing.

The process of transformation proceeds on its journey when you follow the Call to deeper and deeper levels of energetic experience. In a blink of an eye, feel yourself standing on the mountain top you so laboriously struggled to climb. Perspective shifts. Behold before you a new vista, a new world filled with the infinite and eternal possibility of the universe. Feel uplifted, energized, experiencing balance. Know you are whole and complete, powerful and capable. You are transformation. Joyfully, you are ready for the next mountain top, ready to take the next step on your journey.

Thus, the process of embracing breakthrough begins by embracing being within attentive focus of an inside-out perspective. Through being, allow self the opportunity to embrace choice consciously. In the face of fear and feeling unworthy, don't react, instead follow the threads of knowing and bravely explore the nature of your impending transformational breakthrough:

No matter what the Call maybe. No matter the why of following. No matter the preparation or the initiation. In each moment of the journey, life happens, shift happens, the unexpected happens. In each moment of life, find your truth.

By following the fear of breakdown into a focus on doing you will miss the emerging possibilities of breakthrough into a new way of being. Doing is not the end game of the spiritual journey. Instead, *how* you are in each moment of living is the journey. Ultimately, it is in the *how* that transformation occurs, and you move through, being intact.

In this moment, turn attention to heart's depth, and ask self or the Akashic Records:

1. In the face of transformation, in this moment, what is my truth?
2. Where do I feel balance?
3. What knowing do I have that serves me?
4. Where is this motion leading me?

As the journey continues, I affirm:

I step into the river and lay my body down.

I step into the river and let my soul go free.

I step into the river and the river is me.

30

THE GIFT OF FEAR

The paradox of the spiritual journey is the journey is not about getting to good. Instead, it is understanding that good is a limiting label. Instead, the jewels of the journey are often hidden in the most unexpected of places. I have come to think of them as gifts, offerings which surprisingly support the best of my being and becoming if I will step beyond fear and truly experience the best of me no longer hidden by fear and self-judgment.

In this journey of life, there is always a choice about what to feel and to do, to think and to love, to fear and to release. Realistically, the spiritual journey is not always pleasant and there is much which incites fear. Worry, anxiety, stress are all reasonable by-products of efforts to be conscious of intention and integrity, to live life in the present moment with the openness and flexibility of the beginner.

Yet, with this personal awareness also comes the realization of all that can be released and changed. Harder to manage is the pressing feeling of the unrecognizable and the irrational. Often the result of trauma buried deep, these feelings begin to percolate upwards, pushing for attention and resolution. Some can be full of the kind of fear which feels hard to manage and harder to re-suppress.

In transformation, you are asked to risk everything. Transformation asks self to open completely in order to shift and transform. Fear emerges as a natural result. Reasonably, self tries to turn from the fear, avoiding if possible, denying if necessary. But avoidance and denial do not eliminate, only delay.

The best way to deal with fear: look at the fear feelings squarely on and acknowledge, here and now. Acknowledge the most likely source of fear is not that you are incapable or unworthy, but paradoxically, that you are powerful beyond measure.

The gift of fear is a vision of your deepest being. Releasing whatever no longer serves creates an opening to glimpse the deeper parts of being, soul, and connection with All That Is. It's the *Dalai Lama Moment*: the moment when, in humble truth, you claim self as wholely and divinely connected with the vast amazing greatness of All That Is. You are more like the Dalai Lama than you might ever care to admit.

As resistance releases, allow self to feel your power within all creation, allow self to touch the depth of being and the height of soul. Finally, allow self the full recognition that, just like beloved teachers, you, too, are powerful beyond measure. The fear is that if the only path to claim this truth is through an ego-driven grab for power over all. Making this claim may feel selfish, may feel that you are unleashing within a force of domination, greed or ruin.

However, stop, breathe, and consider. Now see beyond fear and the worries anchored in the yet-to-arrive future that another more worthy possibility is available. In the stillness between breath in and breath out, look into your heart and ask for truth. Ask: If I accept the deepest, most powerful part of who I am will I become maniacal and greedy for power over others? If the answer is yes, then more work lies ahead for you. Though the reality for most is that the fear of power is generated by the ego's desire to control and willingly deny self-determination.

Accepting the depth of your divine connection can be done humbly by simply accepting truth. This process does not require you to "do" anything. Instead, admit to self your essential nature and allow self to become aware step-by-step of your deepest being. Allow yourself this understanding and vision because the resistance is dishonest, out of integrity, and untruthful. Acknowledging depth of connection is simply an acknowledgment of who you are in this moment and who you are now becoming. Nothing else is asked, nothing else is required. Stand in truth and claim all of you.

In this moment, turn attention to heart's depth, and ask self or the Akashic Records:

1. What is my deepest fear?
2. How can I release this fear?
3. How does my fear of the unknown hold me back from risk?
4. What is the depth of my being?

As the journey continues, I affirm:

I affirm that fear has no place in my life.

I open my heart to the best of me.

31

JOY

J oy is my measure of commitment and permission to live my life fully and in alignment with my heart. In subtle moments as the sun dances in through the window of my soul. Or the forest lifts my awareness of connection. I feel joy. I live joy. I am joy.

Joy is the soul's balance. Joy is the tune played by the being conscious of balance within. Joy flows when intention and knowing meet in awareness of the unlimited motion of this moment. As resonance with balance at center, joy embraces body, emotion, and heart. Joy brings calm and peace as well as excitement and exuberance. Joy is a response within to the energetic shift of the moment — a resonance similar to the tuning of a guitar. Joy sings of wholeness, bodily-felt awareness of synchronicity, of the rightness of the moment. To feel joy, respond to this shift within the entire energy field of being. Feel self rise above parts into a harmonic sense of unity with self and with All That Is.

From a spiritual perspective, joy is considered a highly desired quality of being because of its ability to indicate balance. Joy is embraced not because it diverts attention from your spiritual-physical being, but exactly because of how it engages attention towards balance and integration of the spiritual and physical. The experience of joy is also the experience of balance of personal power, truth, integrity, and intention. The bubbly dance of joy brings attention to the best launching point for all thought, feeling, and activity in life. Living life in joy frees you to view fear, expectation, and blame from a more empowering vantage point.

In joy, there is less resistance to move beyond what no longer serves, releasing worn-out stories, empowered to make new choices, and move in new directions. Joy is a light to brighten the path and a guide of balance and clarity. Joy is experienced in the release of blocks and the move forward with less stumbling and more confidence. In balance is freedom to follow your dance of joy.

At the center of joy is the peace of soul and a song which brightly illuminates the soul's path. In joy, peace fills the moment. In joy, calm quiets the mind. In joy, exuberance fires the heart. In joy, life is full. In joy, love is present. In joy, being and becoming connect clearly within you in this moment. In joy, feel fully alive, ready to embrace the twists and turns of the journey.

The Ah-ha! moment of transformation ignites joy, illuminating the soul's path of balance. The experience of joy in this moment of shift can be felt as transformation itself. An experience sometimes so intense that the sense of joy can feel like a complete transmutation, as you let go of any sense of the "old" you. The joy of transformation cleanses of ill-serving beliefs and stories. Stripped to the bone of your soul, this joy can catch you unaware of the life-changing shift. The intensity of joy can make it difficult to discern whether the experience is breakdown or breakthrough.

However, sometimes transformation and its attendant sense of joy can be so invigorating, so uplifting, the biggest danger is the temptation to stay put in this feel-good place. The sense of powerful change leads to the desire to stay on the mountain top with all the others who experienced the powerful shift with you. The communal experience of transformation can create its own language alien to those who have not had the same life-shifting opportunity. You want the joy to last forever, You believe if you stay on the mountain with your fellows you can get your desire to last forever, sustaining unchanged the powerful surge of the transformational moment.

But freezing the journey within transformative energy will not serve the path of your soul. You want to fully embrace and experience transformation and all its joy, knowing, and realization. The point of the journey to the mountain top is not to find a resting spot but to find the next valley leading to the next mountain top. The journey brings you to the mountain for understanding and a glimpse of the next part of your path. Spiritual travelers learn that it is not the destination—the *what*—that is important. The wise traveler comes to understand through tender learning and confusion that the spiritual journey is about the *how*—the journey itself. Sticking to the mountain top either out of fear of the unknown or the desire to remain within joy forever brings the journey to an unneeded halt. Standing on the mountain top, transformation brings the clarity that joy continues taking the next step. In this peak experience, you understand now is the time to take the next step and see the journey to the end. The joy of transformation sings the balance of soul and shows how to continue your life's path. In Joy!

In this moment, turn attention to heart's depth, and ask self or the Akashic Records:

1. How does my awareness of balance help me connect with joy?
2. How do expectation, blame, fear or judgment affect or interfere with my joy?
3. How can I feel joy in my heart?

As the journey continues, I affirm:

I open my heart to the flow and feel the joy of ALL.

32

THE DYNAMICS OF TRANSFORMATION

B eholding the mountain peak can be both empowering and overwhelming.

At this point, the journey can seem both too short and too long. You can feel ready and unprepared, thrilled and petrified. Engaging with life as spiritual practice provides a foundation for depth of understanding and a framework for reflection and awareness of truth. While the Call heralds the motion of spirit, transformation is an embracing of the guidance of spirit within the mystery of life and All That Is. The spiritual journey offers perspective, helps process the shift, and understand the direction of your path. Transformation aids vision within life and guides self within truth. Without transformation, growth is stagnant, and learning fails to innovate.

Transformation spirals the journey into new dimensions of vision and truth. Transformation embraces the dynamic and lifts vision of self into a new level of soul guidance and spirit connection. Transformation doesn't bring you home. Instead transformation finds home in this moment of truth, open to the flow of guidance emerging from the interweaving of heart and soul, mind and body.

Transformation is always a new embracing all of who you were, are now, and will become.

In this moment, the journey may also shift and re-focus, giving entrance to new flows of knowing, motion, and intention. The story of your soul opens dynamically to inscribing awareness in this moment, giving voice to soul's guidance, and illuminating the infinite and eternal possibilities of all that is you. Transformation launches you from this moment to the next by opening you to the guidance of spirit, the guidance of divine source, the guidance of All That Is. Open your heart, breathe in, and step into your soul's beautiful mystery, transformed.

In this moment, turn attention to heart's depth, and ask self or the Akashic Records:

1. What does the mountain peak offer the journey of my life?
2. What is home for me?
3. What is my soul's mystery?

As the journey continues, I affirm:

I stand transformed within the beauty of my soul.

33

SUMMARY

STEP FOUR: TRANSFORMATION

Walk, walk. Trudge, trudge. Back-up. Walk. Drag, halt, drag. Turnaround. Walk, walk, walk.

A-HA!

Release, shift.

At the mountain top: new view!

Temptation to stay put, feels so good!

New vista beckons.

Down the mountain to the next valley.

Time to finish the journey.

Trusting to allow inner truth to guide.

In Joy!

In this moment, turn attention to heart's depth, and ask self or the Akashic Records:

1. Where do I experience pain (emotional, physical, spiritual, etc.)?
2. Focus on one point: What is this pain about? What does this pain want to pass on to me now?
3. How do I experience integrity in my body? In my thoughts? In my feelings?
4. How do I confuse *being* with *doing*?
5. In my life, where do I experience light and where do I experience darkness?
6. In this moment how do I experience my body, mind, heart, and soul?

As the journey continues, I affirm:

In joy, I embrace the clear vision of each transformative moment in my life.

STEP FIVE: INTEGRATION

HEART AND MIND AS ONE WITH SPIRIT

Gathering not as many but as One.

Feeling the waves of the boundlessness as ripples through all.

Begin again.

Student and master are one.

Hear the call quicken and the urge to travel emerge.

The one within The ONE.

34

INTEGRATION

From the mountaintop of transformation, the next step brings you into the valley of daily life. This final step of the spiritual path, Integration, is both necessary for the completion of the journey and for empowering an inner sense of truth and trust.

Integration brings together heart and mind, physical and spiritual, within and without. Integration asks that you step forward with all of who you are, imperfections and dreams, warts, scars, and hard-won understandings of life's truths. Integration requests ALL of you — all joy, awareness, fear, challenge. Integration presents the opportunity to weave all parts together in whatever manner may serve truth in this moment.

Relying on the knowing gained from the transformative moment, integration guides toward weaving this new learning into the fabric of everyday life. Integration defies the temptation of separation and division, and instead embraces all. Instead of a hermit hidden at the peak of transformation, integration brings you fully into this moment willingly embracing and claiming all of your being here, now.

The spiritual journey is not about ridding life of problems and injustices. Instead, the journey empowers the truth of deepest being to inspire and enliven each moment. Then, through choice, you may transmute the old, outdated patterns and habits of life. Choosing your experience and your stories offers the opportunity to live consciously from the truth of heart and the infinite power of being. Integration completes the journey, readying you to begin the next.

Broadly, integration is the process of weaving together the unique flow that you are with the learning and knowing available from all aspects and opportunities of the journey. Integration is finding self fully present to experience here and now. Integration is coming to terms with the fact that no matter the spiritual experience, life goes on, requiring attention to the mundane details such as laundry, groceries, and cleaning.

Spiritual "awakening" does not elevate to some special, rarefied plane of existence. Quite the opposite, the opportunity of integration is to make the transformative experience of the mountain top part of everyday life.

The challenge of integration is to live from the knowing gained through all the steps bringing you to this moment: transformation, initiation, preparation, and the Call. The spiritual journey joins spiritual and physical in a supportive, integrated whole allowing you the freedom to choose your point of view and your responses to life's flow. Integration helps utilize the everyday, such as laundry, groceries, and cleaning, as life's spiritual practice.

Additionally, integration is not perfection of action, thought, or feeling. Integration is the evolving, interconnecting *awareness* of your actions, thoughts, and feelings. Integration, as much as the previous steps in your journey, relies on your attention, awareness, and observation as your way of being and living. Integration strives to create action from conscious choice rather than from blind reaction to expectation, blame, fear, and judgment.

Integration helps shift into awareness of balance. In the journey, find you are not chasing balance into form. Rather there is a letting go of whatever blocks awareness of balance. Balance always is. The spiritual journey helps you remember and embrace balance, allowing balance to find you and unfold for you in the moment as is. No longer dominated by the inflexibility of ego, you have come to know and feel balance within. The guidance of truth is found through the support of intention, integrity, present moment, and beginner's mind. Awareness of balance and of truth help you discern your next step whatever that step may be.

In this moment, turn attention to heart's depth, and ask self or the Akashic Records:

1. What in my daily life holds me back from the fullness of my spiritual journey?
2. What frees me to fully embrace integration as my next step?
3. How may I release my desire for perfection?
4. How does beginner's mind support full integration in this moment?

As the journey continues, I affirm:

Ready for whatever is for me now, I trust myself to find my path even if I can't see the way.

35

THE NEXT BEGINNING

Here's a crucial concept: open your mind and heart to the understanding that everyone is trying to do their best.

The issue is that the definition of "best" varies greatly. Whether someone has the same beliefs, operates at similar vibration, speaks the same heart language, or paints the world with the same brush as you or not – none of these are reasons to judge, or accept, or reject. When dealing with the vast unknown of the spiritual journey, finding comfort in similar perspectives is understandable. But to insist on similarities in order to determine the "right people" for friends is limiting and ultimately harmful to you. The concept of Namaste is not a yardstick for judgment, but support and encouragement to find connection within the essential truth and beautiful heart of another regardless of outward appearance. The gift of integration is the awareness of infinite connection of you with ALL.

In retrospect, on the mountaintop of transformation, there is little direct challenge to the wonderful new you. Yet, when you step into integration, assistance is needed to complete this cycle by figuring out how to incorporate transformation into everyday life.

Shifts and changes are felt within. Personal choices and reactions have shifted. Situations do not trigger as before. Calm and quiet feel more natural. Then comes the yappy dog, the annoying neighbor, and the bossy employer, all challenges to a perfected state. Those wanting to avoid the mess and trial of integration will respond by wanting to return to the mountain top where these annoyances can presumably be more easily handled or, better yet, avoided all together. Perhaps, hanging out with those who you believe understand your experience are much preferred to those who you think obviously don't understand.

However, in its rightful place in the cycle of learning, integration holds as its promise not an end but a view of the next beginning. In integration, do not hold self on the banks of the river of life where illusion and denial tempt ego. Instead, follow your heart into the full flow of the river seeking the mainstream where the water is the swiftest. Whether you metaphorically sink or swim is not the concern. In integration, challenge self to seek the act of full engagement, full yielding, full embracing. Guide your heart to continually seek limits to transcend and wholeness to claim. Failure is only failure if you do not try.

The choice of integration emerges by allowing self the opportunity for reflection and awareness independent from ego's demand for retreat or pointless reaction. Resistance to integration shows up in the contradictory request, "How can I make my life only about my learning?" Whereas integration as a natural process begins when you ask, "How can I make my journey's learning part of my life?" Integration is inclusive of ALL. Resistance to integration is limiting, exclusive – and avoids challenge. Integration looks for opportunities to try out new learning.

Resistance to integration appears because the ego still believes that the point of the spiritual journey is to get rid of the ugly spots of life and live in perfection. The inflexibility of ego demands no less. The rigidness of ego also demands that you hold yourself as special and better than those who didn't reach the transformational peak with you. Ego mistakenly equates balance with perfection.

The realness of integration calmly challenges these ego assumptions, moving easily without the dominance and control of ego. Ultimately the choice is yours. Resistance holds self back from the truth of your infinite and eternal nature. Instead, in joy and in truth, step fully into the river of your life.

In this moment, turn attention to heart's depth, and ask self or the Akashic Records:

1. How am I afraid to begin?
2. What can I receive in the moment which helps me take my next step?
3. How can I make my journey's learning part of my life?
4. What am I holding on to which no longer serves me?

As the journey continues, I affirm:

As I let go of the unnecessary and the unessential, I see that my inner essence is my truest guide.

36

EVERYWHERE IS SACRED SPACE

F*or me sacred space shows up primarily within two possibilities. First, when I become aware that I have entered sacred space. The sanctuary of a church, the hallowed ground of a memorial, the altar of a shrine – places created by others as sacred space. The second is the deep awareness that I hold sacred space for myself with clear intention and in each moment. Standing on the top of the mountain, on a path through old forest, at the beach – the experience brings my inner awareness to feel and embrace my experience as sacred, as connected, as foundation. The macro and the micro, the implicit and the explicit. I see me see ALL. I feel me feel ALL. As sacred space, I am the experience of ALL.*

The primary spiritual concept of integration is sacred space. The challenge is understanding what is and is not sacred space. The opportunity is learning to live your life as sacred space.

Sacred space is created within when the spiritual and physical components of balance yield to and integrate with the transcendent nature of universal life force, the creative motion of All That Is. Universal life force animates the physical and spiritual dimensions, allowing you to participate in this moment as a multi-dimensional being. Universal life force brings the miraculous, the unexpected, and the unknown. By yielding the spiritual and the physical to this transcendence, you allow the integration of heart and mind, body and soul, guided by balance within and divine connection with All That Is.

In sacred space, you declare wholeness and willingness to live in awareness of divine connection and the transcendence which offers guidance from within heart and soul. You create your reality here and now through the flow of your choice.

However, it is the unpredictable flow of universal life force which supports the next step toward highest expression. To live life within sacred space, you yield control by your mind to the truth in your heart, stepping you know not where, yet trusting in the unfailing support of All That Is. Gather together the harvest of your journey: beginner's mind, present moment focus, intention, and integrity. Allow their integration to find sacred space within. In the sacred space of integration, unity within always is.

Sacred space requires beginner's mind because this openness to unlimited possibility creates within self an expanded opening to awareness of All That Is and the motion of the divine on all levels. By moving beyond the limitations of assumptions, allow self the opportunity to embrace life within infinite possibility. Claim space, sacred in its willingness to open to the infinite and eternal potential of divine connection.

Sacred space also requires this present moment to create a foundation within the infinite and eternal All That Is. The truth of sacred space can make itself known as a fully present and focused witness, here and now. Focus trapped in either the past or the future weakens awareness, blocking the ability to give attention and observe the process of life, to make choices, and to continue the journey.

Truth as the strong foundation of sacred space becomes the creative foundation for all experience of the spiritual journey. Without truth, sacred space is weakened, fading from attention, observation, and awareness. In sacred space, intention serves as guide within the flow of All That Is. Intention provides the focal point which shifts learning and awareness of you in this moment of being. Intention connects you with awareness of truth.

In sacred space, integrity aids in the awareness of balance within the infinite and eternal foundation of energy that is each and every human being. Integrity is the conduit of truth and trust within this divine connection. Integrity is the flow of spirit leading to clearer understanding of highest expression, here, now, always.

Sacred space is not a special physical place only available to the initiated or the anointed. Sacred space is the circle of truth you establish through the support of these four primary concepts as the touchstones of your spiritual journey. Together these touchstones form your circle as sacred space, enabling your existence to experience truth across the entirety of body, mind, heart, and soul. Together these touchstones also support attention, observation, and awareness of the infinite and eternal experience of divine connection.

Sacred space is the breath of your life and the sustenance of your soul. Sacred space is your life and your joy. Sacred space lives in your heart and fills your words with connection, learning, and infinite knowing. Sacred space is you choosing to live life as divine connection. In love and light, your life's journey is sacred space within the infinite and eternal All That Is.

All spiritual practice, across all spiritual and religious traditions, intentionally invokes sacred space. The focus and intention of spiritual ritual is to aid in consciously calling on the presence of the divine. Lighting candles, burning incense, reciting holy manuscript, kneeling in penitence, meditating and prayer—are all at their common foundation efforts to accept the guidance and support of divine sacred space.

In your journey, you will discover the ritual elements which support your ability to establish and live within sacred space. Much like balance, which always is, sacred space is not about creating the non-existent. Rather sacred space is about clearing self to be able to find within awareness of its presence. Ritual may assist in finding a path. However, beware ritual which becomes rigid and demanding. Incense and candles are not sacred space, only reminders of what lies within heart and soul if you take the opportunity to give attention and observe.

Reflection is key.

- Observe your process and your responses to your process.
- Observe what works and what triggers.
- Observe where flow moves easily and where resistance steps forward.
- Observe where you have choice and what deflects your attention from the gap between reaction and action through choice.

Reflection is observation free from censure and condemnation. Reflection observes and allows the learning of the moment to guide towards clarity and truth.

Within sacred space, blame and fear can be accepted and released, here and now. Remain conscious of you as sacred space first by opening to truth and love. Now trust can lead to your truth. Step eagerly into the ebb and flow of life as beginner's mind transforms *I know* to **I LEARN**.

Breathe.

Observe.

Reflect.

Trust.

As sacred space, you are ready for whatever is for you in this moment.

———

In this moment, turn attention to heart's depth, and ask self or the Akashic Records:

1. How does breath bring me to awareness of sacred space?
2. How does observation bring me to awareness of sacred space?
3. How does reflection bring me to awareness of sacred space?
4. How does truth bring me to awareness of sacred space?

———

As the journey continues, I affirm:

Within Sacred Space, I am ready for whatever is for me now.

———

37

THE DYNAMICS OF INTEGRATION

J *ust be. Mmmm.... How? I think to myself.*

What I know now is that to experience BE is not about the perfect execution of a defined set of steps. Instead as you set off on your journey, you take a step and then another until one day, your attention brings you to the awareness, "I BE." Not a repeated formula, a juried award of excellence, or an identified number of steps. Simply a moment of perception about self, for self, from self, I BE.

There is a place within self which will always identify with the highest expression of who you are and can become. Learning to feel this essence, at center, aids in feeling solid in truth and in your ability to get to truth. In this place feel balance, peace, and joy. In this place, feel your wholeness. In this place, feel the sacred expression of your being and the ability to connect and move from this sacred space.

The essence of your spiritual journey helps in learning to connect with center more often than not, regardless of the circumstances of life. Your journey is a coming home to the integrated hearth of being, a focal point of the transformed nature of heart and mind, body and soul. The connection allows you to touch and be enveloped by the warmth of this your sacred space.

Every step brings you here. Every experience helps release the blocks of fear, doubt, blame, judgment, and expectation. Every story becomes an interweaving of truth and support. Every story empowers additional release and expanded understanding of your dynamic self. To behold self uncluttered and unfettered is humbling. To allow self to breathe in spirit's guidance and to answer the Call is liberating. To let guidance show you a new way through the unknown is the entirety of the spiritual journey.

Integrated within the perspective of the journey allows you to feel and respond in wholeness to your life. Not because you are perfect, but because you have learned to stand in awe of your ability to witness the infinite and eternal flow of All That Is. As witness, the sacred fills the space of your being and you feel connection, compassion, and love for all. At one with self, at one with all being, home in wholeness, in joy and love. You begin and end your journey filled with the light of your soul and the music of All That Is. In Joy!

In this moment, turn attention to heart's depth, and ask self or the Akashic Records:

1. How am I connected with All That Is?
2. How does my body, mind, heart, and soul integrate with All That Is?
3. What is the story of my soul?
4. What is the story of my spiritual journey?

As the journey continues, I affirm:

As my heart shows me the steps of my path, I go willingly into the light.

38

SUMMARY

STEP FIVE: INTEGRATION

L ife is the best spiritual workshop ever.

To be present in this moment, especially in the face of fear, trauma, and pain is a challenge. Intention, integrity, and trust are also daily challenges especially when balance seems to be nothing but struggle and awareness is dimmed by the course of life's events. Giving self a gap between reaction and choice allows time to reflect and then respond with intention and clarity. Take this opportunity not because it guarantees the removal of pain, obstacle, or dissatisfaction but because the opportunity empowers learning about self and how you may consciously attend to life.

Living deeply requires deep practice and a willingness to honestly and lovingly self-correct when the road gets bumpy. This is why integration as the fifth and final step of the spiritual journey is so vitally important. Integration is a weaving together of everything that has preceded this last step. Integration helps make sense of all that has been learned within the context of daily life. Integration asks you to be present to the world you live in, working to overcome whatever tends to make you feel separate from, alone, or alienated. Integration claims sacred, divine nature and calls you to give attention, to observe, and to be aware.

You are this amazing, integrated person, capable beyond measure, loving and lovable without limits. Integration provides empowerment to take another step, to experience another journey without being certain of where you will go or what you will learn. Sometimes this next step is clear, sometimes not so much. However, the clarity and the trust which emerges with your conscious attention to your journey provides the support you need to let go of the demand for perfection and guaranteed results.

You move forward because you trust yourself even if you can't see the road ahead. You take that next step because you have become a willing traveler, confident that somehow the Call will be made clear. You take the next step because you have a sense that you can figure out what preparations are needed and that you will be able to receive the gifts of the journey. You know that in responding to your journey and opportunities to learn, that you will be able to take in the shifts that come no matter how powerful or subtle they may be.

You journey, you realize, because this is how you experience the depths of your soul and feel the deep love of your heart. You journey because to do otherwise would be a deep betrayal of your authentic essence, a lie to self. You journey, with trust, with a sense of truth in this moment, in this moment of balance with All That Is. You journey because the journey is your life.

In this moment, turn attention to heart's depth, and ask self or the Akashic Records:

1. What can I do to create sacred space in my life?
2. How can I integrate the learning of my journey into my life?
3. What am I grateful for in my life?

4. What challenges my balance and my truth?
5. What have I learned on my journey?
6. How do I begin again?

As the journey continues, I affirm:

I am always open to learn as I take the next step on my journey.

READY TO LEARN MORE?

T hank you so much for reading this book!

I am passionate about supporting you in your journey to find clarity and feel confident about who you are and who you can become.

For me, I write to share my truth in hopes you feel confident in finding and trusting your truth.

If you'd like to continue learning one-on-one, visit my website: **CherylMarlene.com**

Find a wide variety of spiritual consciousness and metaphysical articles, workshops, and workbooks at SpiritualDeepDive.com — when others skim, we dive!

If you would like to learn to access the Akashic Records with me, you have these options:

- **Books**: particularly *Akashic Records Masterclass*, shares how to open your Akashic Records and the Akashic Records of both human and non-human energy.

- *__Akashic Record Insights__*: weekly practices, workshops, workbooks plus a repository of information to expand your Akashic Records journey. Visit AkashicRecordsArchive.com

- **Akashic Records Intensive**: When you are ready, with me as your in-person guide, to go beyond stereotype into learning within the powerful depths of the sacred mysteries of the Akashic Records. Learn more and apply on my website.

These are all great options. Everything you need is there. Plus, you can add one-on-one student mentorship session when connecting directly with me calls to you.

Know that unlike a lot of places, all workshops, and especially the *Akashic Records Intensive*, are done in-person with me via Zoom. Videos are simply supplemental.

Whatever path your journey may take, may you experience and live within intrinsic truth, trust, and self-worth.

BELIEVE. Laugh. Learn. Love. Be. Become. Always.

In Joy!

Cheryl

ABOUT CHERYL

www.CherylMarlene.com

Cheryl Marlene is a pioneering guide in spiritual consciousness and the Akashic Records, blazing a new path for seekers ready to move beyond superficial answers. Her work is for those who desire unvarnished truth, deep transformation, and a profound connection to personal power.

A mystic, futurist, and trailblazer, Cheryl expands the Akashic Records beyond outdated myths into a living, dynamic spiritual practice, uniting divine and human consciousness in profound healing. Through one-on-one Akashic Record sessions, research, and future-driven business consulting, she helps clients and visionaries uncover their soul's wisdom and embrace their fullest potential.

As the creator of the *Akashic Records Intensive,* the most comprehensive Akashic Records training, and author of *Akashic Records Masterclass,* Cheryl challenges the limits of what's possible in spiritual innovation. Her students and clients know her as relatable, insightful, and unafraid of the raw and real aspects of deep work.

When she's not writing, Cheryl is on the hiking trail, listening to nature's wisdom and exploring the heartbeat of the mountain.

Through her journey, she has distilled her intention for life to these seven words:

BELIEVE. Laugh. Learn. Love. Be. Become. Always.

CherylMarlene.com

Bookstore.CherylMarlene.com

AkashicRecordInsights.com

SpiritualDeepDive.com

ALSO BY CHERYL MARLENE

Bookstore.CherylMarlene.com

Akashic Records Masterclass

Masterclass includes these four books which may also be purchased separately:

What are the Akashic Records?

Open Your Akashic Records

Open the Akashic Records for Other

500 Questions to Ask the Akashic Records

The New Akashic Records

Akashic Records: Gemstone Guardians

Gemstone Guardians Journal

How to Navigate the Five Steps of Your Spiritual Journey

Soul Compass: Trusting Inner Truth to Navigate Life's Uncertainties

Soul Compass Companion Journal

Spiritual Deep Dive Workshop-in-a-Book Series:

Understanding Doubt

Mastering Self Responsibility

Authenticity and the Soul

www.ingramcontent.com/pod-product-compliance
Lightning Source LLC
LaVergne TN
LVHW051059080426
835508LV00019B/1972